**Eliete Canesi Morino**
Graduada pela Pontifícia Universidade Católica de São Paulo (PUC-SP)
em Língua e Literatura Inglesa e Tradução e Interpretação.
Especialização em Língua Inglesa pela International Bell School of London.
Pós-graduada em Metodologia da Língua Inglesa pela Faculdade de Tecnologia e Ciência.
Atuou como professora na rede particular de ensino e em projetos comunitários.

**Rita Brugin de Faria**
Graduada pela Faculdade de Arte Santa Marcelina
e pela Faculdade Paulista de Arte.
Especialização em Língua Inglesa pela International Bell School of London.
Pós-graduada em Metodologia da Língua Inglesa pela Faculdade de Tecnologia e Ciência.
Especialista em alfabetização, atuou como professora e coordenadora
pedagógica nas redes pública e particular de ensino.

**editora scipione**

**Presidência:** Mario Ghio Júnior
**Direção editorial:** Lidiane Vivaldini Olo
**Gerência editorial:** Viviane Carpegiani
**Gestão de área:** Tatiany Renó (Anos Iniciais)
**Edição:** Mariangela Secco (coord.), Ana Lucia Militello
**Planejamento e controle de produção:** Flávio Matuguma, Juliana Batista, Felipe Nogueira e Juliana Gonçalves
**Revisão:** Kátia Scaff Marques (coord.), Brenda T. M. Morais, Cláudia Virgílio, Daniela Lima, Malvina Tomáz e Ricardo Miyake
**Arte:** André Gomes Vitale (ger.), Catherine Saori Ishihara (coord.), Christine Getschko (edição de arte)
**Iconografia e tratamento de imagem:** Denise Durand Kremer (ger.), Claudia Bertolazzi (coord.), Fernando Cambetas (pesquisa), Fernanda Crevin (tratamento de imagens)
**Licenciamento de conteúdos de terceiros:** Roberta Bento (gerente); Jenis Oh (coord.); Liliane Rodrigues e Flávia Zambon (analistas); Raísa Maris Reina (assist.)
**Ilustrações:** Marcos de Mello (Aberturas de unidade), AMJ Studio, Ari Nicolesi, Ilustra Cartoon, Marimbando e Sirayama
**Design:** Gláucia Correa Koller (ger.), Flávia Dutra e Gustavo Vanini (proj. gráfico e capa), Erik Taketa (pós-produção)
**Ilustração de capa:** Estúdio Luminos

Todos os direitos reservados por Somos Sistemas de ensino S.A.
Avenida Paulista, 901, 6º andar – Bela Vista
São Paulo – SP – CEP 01310-200
http://www.somoseducacao.com.br

Dados Internacionais de Catalogação na Publicação (CIP)

```
Morino, Eliete Canesi
   Marcha Criança : Língua Inglesa : 1º ao 5º ano /
Eliete Canesi Morino, Rita Brugin. -- 3. ed. -- São
Paulo : Scipione, 2020.
   (Coleção Marcha Criança ; vol. 1 ao 5)

Bibliografia

1. Língua inglesa (Ensino fundamental) - Anos iniciais
I. Título II. Brugin, Rita III. Série

                                         CDD 372.652
20-1102
```

Angélica Ilacqua - Bibliotecária - CRB-8/7057

**2023**
Código da obra CL 745887
CAE 721146 (AL) / 721147 (PR)
ISBN 9788547403096 (AL)
ISBN 9788547403102 (PR)
2ª edição
5ª impressão
De acordo com a BNCC.

Impressão e acabamento: Vox Gráfica

Uma publicação SOMOS EDUCAÇÃO

Com ilustrações de **Marcos de Mello**, seguem abaixo os créditos das fotos utilizadas nas aberturas de Unidade:

**UNIDADE 1: Regador:** Nataliia K/Shutterstock, **Jarra:** krolya25/Shutterstock, **Canteiro:** Derek Harris Photography/Shutterstock, **Manteiga:** Aquarius Studio/Shutterstock, **Suporte com bolo:** boitano/Shutterstock, **Casa:** Anton Mezinov/Shutterstock, **Cesta de pães:** Vasilevich Aliaksandr/Shutterstock, **Jarra com suco:** Anton Starikov/Shutterstock.

**UNIDADE 2: Sofá:** Nina Mikryukova/Shutterstock, **Cozinha:** New Africa/Shutterstock, **Interior de casa:** Tom Peppiatt/Shutterstock, **Escola:** James R. Martin/Shutterstock, **Gramado:** Theerapol Pongkangsananan/Shutterstock, **Cama:** Ljupco Smokovski/Shutterstock, **Piscina:** tarczas/Shutterstock, **Sala de aula:** maroke/Shutterstock.

**UNIDADE 3: Fachada do shopping:** Thomas Trompeter/Shutterstock, **Fachada do pet shop:** Derick Hudson/Shutterstock, **Fachada da livraria:** Peter Moulton/Shutterstock, **Caminhão:** Siwakorn1933/Shutterstock, **Fachada de Fast Food:** Eric Lysenko/Shutterstock, **Porta da loja de brinquedos:** Martin Good/Shutterstock, **Carro:** Maksim Toome/Shutterstock, **Ônibus:** Tang Yan Song/Shutterstock, **Avião:** phive/Shutterstock, **Motocicleta:** MiloVad/Shutterstock, **Fachada da loja de itens para Surf:** Kagan Kaya/Shutterstock, **Trem:** GE_4530/Shutterstock.

**UNIDADE 4: Folhagem:** evrymmnt/Shutterstock, **Tronco de árvore:** PhilipYb Studio/Shutterstock, **Árvore:** Chansom Pantip/Shutterstock, **Cacto:** Chansom Pantip/Shutterstock, **Folha:** Mari Franz/Shutterstock, **Tronco de árvore 2:** PhilipYb Studio/Shutterstock, **Folhagem 2:** TKGGP/Shutterstock, **Canoa:** frankie's/Shutterstock.

# APRESENTAÇÃO

Querido aluno, querida aluna,

Quanto mais cedo começamos a estudar uma segunda língua, mais simples e fácil é aprendê-la.

Com a coleção **Marcha Criança - Língua Inglesa**, você descobrirá que o inglês já faz parte do dia a dia, e esperamos que você tenha prazer em aprender esse idioma, tão necessário para entender melhor o mundo em que vivemos.

Aqui você encontra um modo divertido de aprender por meio de diversas atividades, como colagens, desenhos, pinturas, dramatizações, jogos, canções e muito mais!

Participe com entusiasmo das aulas e aproveite esta oportunidade que o professor e esta coleção propiciam: aprender inglês de maneira bastante instigante e motivadora.

*Good job!*

As autoras

Marcos de Mello/Arquivo da editora

# KNOW YOUR BOOK

Veja a seguir como seu livro está organizado.

### JOIN THE CIRCLE!
Você e os colegas terão a oportunidade de conversar sobre a cena apresentada e a respeito do que já sabem sobre o tema da unidade.

### UNIT
Seu livro está organizado em quatro unidades temáticas, com aberturas em páginas duplas. Cada unidade tem duas lições. As aberturas de unidade são compostas dos seguintes boxes:

### LET'S LEARN!
Aqui você vai encontrar a lista dos conteúdos que serão estudados na unidade.

### LISTEN AND SAY
Esta seção tem o propósito de fazer você observar e explorar a cena de abertura da lição. Permite também que você entre em contato com as estruturas que serão trabalhadas e desenvolva as habilidades auditiva e oral.

### KEY WORDS
Este boxe apresenta nomes de objetos e de partes da cena de abertura que serão estudados ao longo da lição.

### LANGUAGE TIME
Esta seção traz atividades que vão possibilitar que você explore a língua inglesa de forma simples e natural.

### NOW, WE KNOW!
Momento de verificar se os conteúdos foram compreendidos por meio de atividades diversificadas.

## LET'S PRACTICE!

Esta seção propõe atividades para reforçar o que foi estudado na lição. Você vai colocar em prática o que aprendeu nas seções anteriores.

## IT'S YOUR TURN!

Esta seção propõe atividades procedimentais, experiências ou vivências para você aprender na prática o conteúdo estudado.

## TALKING ABOUT...

A seção traz uma seleção de temas para refletir, discutir e aprender mais, capacitando você para atuar no dia a dia com mais consciência!

## REVIEW

Esta seção traz atividades de revisão de cada uma das lições.

## LET'S PLAY!

Atividades lúdicas para que você aprenda enquanto se diverte!

## ≥ Material complementar ≤

## READER

Livro de leitura que acompanha cada volume. A história estimula a imaginação e o conhecimento linguístico, levando você a uma aventura emocionante pelo mundo da literatura.

## GLOSSARY

Traz as palavras-chave em inglês estudadas ao longo deste volume, seguidas da tradução em português.

### Quando você encontrar estes ícones, fique atento!

 In pairs       In groups       Say       Stick       Write

 Draw       Circle       Make an X       Number       Color

 Dot to dot       Match       Listen

# CONTENTS

## UNIT 1 — HOME, SWEET HOME! ......... 8

### ≋ LESSON 1 ≋
**At Home** .................................. 10

Language Points

dining room, garden, garage, laundry room, backyard, window, door

Where is your mom, Tom? / She is in the kitchen. / Oh, she is not here. She is in the bedroom.

### ≋ LESSON 2 ≋
**A Beautiful Garden** .................... 20

Language Points

daisy, butterfly, grass, bee, tree, ladybug, ant, rose

Look at my garden. / Your garden is beautiful, Millie. / Look, a red rose, a white and yellow daisy and... a red and black ladybug!

**Talking About...:**
A Garden in a Plastic Bottle ............ 30

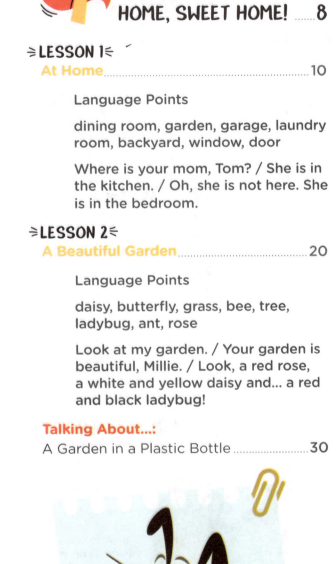

## UNIT 2 — DAILY ROUTINES ......... 32

### ≋ LESSON 3 ≋
**What's for Breakfast?** .................. 34

Language Points

water, toast, cereal, yogurt, French fries, soda, pizza, hot dog

What's for breakfast? / What's for lunch? / We can have something healthy! / What about some chicken with salad?

### ≋ LESSON 4 ≋
**It's Time to Go!** ......................... 44

Language Points

go to sleep, study, play, have lunch, have breakfast, go to school, wake up, eat

What time is it, mom? / It's 7 o'clock. / Let's have breakfast. / Are we late, mom? / Yes, you are. / It's seven thirty!

**It's Your Turn!:**
Let's Make a Meals Record Chart! ............ 54

## UNIT 3 — LIFE IN THE CITY .......... 56

### ⇒ LESSON 5 ⇐
**Talking about Jobs** .......... 58

Language Points

lawyer, engineer, doctor, bus driver, mechanic, postwoman, teacher, baker, policewoman, dentist

What is his job? / Is he a teacher? / No, he is not a teacher. He is a dentist.

### ⇒ LESSON 6 ⇐
**Around the City** .......... 68

Language Points

pet shop, toy store, surf shop, fast food place, play area, bookstore

Where is the new mall? / It is five blocks from here. / How can we get there? / By car/by bus... / Is there a toy store there? / Yes, there is.

**Talking About...:**
The Importance of Each Profession .......... 78

## UNIT 4 — PEOPLE AND NATURE .......... 80

### ⇒ LESSON 7 ⇐
**Save the Animals!** .......... 82

Language Points

blue macaw, manatee, giant panda bear, golden lion tamarin, jaguar, humpback whale, loggerhead sea turtle, gorilla

Is there an animal world channel on TV? / Today there is a program about saving the animals. / There is a cute and fluffy giant panda bear on TV! / We can make a video about giant pandas.

### ⇒ LESSON 8 ⇐
**A Cool Trip!** .......... 92

Language Points

dress, skirt, shorts, jeans, T-shirt, shirt, socks, cap, sneakers, shoes

Let's pack our bags, Lily. Here is your blue dress and your brown shoes. / Tom, your jeans and your sneakers. / Why, Lily? / It is summer.

**It's Your Turn!:**
Let's Make a Pantanal Model! .......... 102

**REVIEW** .......... 104
**LET'S PLAY!** .......... 112
**AUDIO TRANSCRIPT** .......... 120
**GLOSSARY** .......... 122
**SUGGESTIONS FOR STUDENTS** .......... 127
**BIBLIOGRAPHY** .......... 128
**THE FLASH** .......... 129
**STICKERS**

Sirayama/Arquivo da editora

## Let's Learn!
- Family members
- Garden elements and insects
- Subject pronouns
- Possessive adjectives
- Colors
- Where is/are...
- Numbers 0-70

# LESSON 1 — AT HOME

## Listen and say

## Key Words

**1** Look, listen and say.

dining room | garden | garage

## To Learn More

When the British and German colonizers came to the United States, they brought cookies recipes with them. Cookies are flat, sweet cake-like treats.

laundry room · backyard · window · door

# Language Time

**1** Read the chart. Then circle the correct answers.

| Subject Pronouns | I | you | he | she | it | we | you | they |
|---|---|---|---|---|---|---|---|---|
| Verb to Be (Present tense) | am | are | is | is | is | are | are | are |

a) (I / You / He) am Richard.

b) (She / We / He) is my father.

c) (She / They / He) is my mother.

d) (You / We / It) is a beautiful sunflower.

e) (They / We / I) are a big family.

f) Hey, (you / they / he)! Listen to my explanation, please.

g) (We / You / They) have a baby now.

12 twelve

# Now, We Know!

**1** Complete the missing letters of the words.

| B | | D | | O | M |

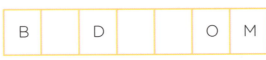

| | I | | I | | R | | M |

| | | I | | I | | O | | |

| K | | C | | | |

| B | | | R | O | |

| | A | | | G | |

| W | | | | O | |

| | | | | R | |

## 2 Match and write sentences.

a) He is in the ✪ ✪ ✪.

b) She is in the ✪ ✪ ✪.

c) They are in the ✪ ✪ ✪.

d) It is in the ✪ ✪ ✪.

a) ................................................................................................................

b) ................................................................................................................

c) ................................................................................................................

d) ................................................................................................................

# Let's Practice!

**1** Write sentences according to the chart.

|   | 1 | 2 | 3 |
|---|---|---|---|
| A | grandma | and | are |
| B | in | teacher | the |
| C | they | grandpa | bedroom |
| D | dining room | girls | kitchen |

a)

| C2 | A2 | A1 | A3 |
|----|----|----|----|
|    |    |    |    |

| B1 | B3 | D1 |
|----|----|----|
|    |    |    |

b)

| B3 | D2 | A3 |
|----|----|----|
|    |    |    |

| B1 | B3 | C3 |
|----|----|----|
|    |    |    |

c)

| C1 | A3 | B1 |
|----|----|----|
|    |    |    |

| B3 | D3 |
|----|----|
|    |    |

**2** Answer the question: What is a floor plan?

a) It is a drawing of the rooms in a house. ☐

b) It is a picture of the outside of a house. ☐

**3** Read the text, look at the floor plans and make an **X**.

> Hello! My name is Amanda and this is my house.
>
> In the floor plan of my house there are three bedrooms. One for my mom and dad, one for my grandma and grandpa and one for me.
>
> There is a big TV in the living room. In front of the house there is a big garage. There is a dining room, a kitchen and two bathrooms. There are a lot of doors and windows in my house.
>
> There is a big tree and a small garden in front of the house. In the back of the house, there is a big backyard too. I love it because I can play with my dog Marley. I love my house. It is big and very comfortable.

a)        b)

☐        ☐

4   Look at the two houses. Circle what is different.

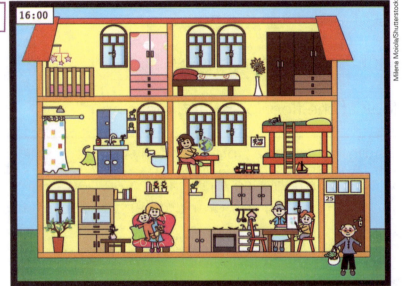

5   Read the sentences and check **YES** or **NO**.

a) In picture A, grandpa is at the front door.   YES ☐   NO ☐

b) In picture B, the girl is in her bedroom.   YES ☐   NO ☐

c) In picture A, grandma is in the kitchen with her grandson.   YES ☐   NO ☐

d) In picture B, the mother and the baby are in the living room.   YES ☐   NO ☐

**6** Draw the floor plan of your dream house.

## Let's Sing!

**Hello, Everybody!**

Where is Lily?
She is in the bathroom.
Where are Tom and Steve?
They are in the kitchen.
Where is Noah?
He is in the living room.
And where are you?
I'm here, in front of you!
Ha!, Ha!, Ha!

## LESSON 2: A BEAUTIFUL GARDEN

### Listen and say

### Key Words

**1** Look, listen and say.

daisy     butterfly     grass     bee

# Language Time

**1** Read the chart. Then complete the sentences below with *a* or *an*.

| Indefinite articles | a | a rose / a daisy |
|---|---|---|
| | an | an ant / an insect |

This is ............ beautiful garden. I can see ............ ant and ............ bee. There are three flowers: ............ yellow, ............ red and ............ blue one. Look, there is ............ beautiful blue butterfly.

**2** Read the examples. Then complete the sentences using *my* or *your*.

| Subject pronouns | Possessive adjectives |
|---|---|
| I | My |
| You | Your |

a)

............ cat Milo is adorable.

b)

Hey, Mike! ............ schoolbag and sneakers are on the floor.

## 3  Listen, point and say the numbers.

| 0 zero | 1 one | 2 two | 3 three | 4 four | 5 five |
|---|---|---|---|---|---|
| 6 six | 7 seven | 8 eight | 9 nine | 10 ten | 11 eleven |
| 12 twelve | 13 thirteen | 14 fourteen | 15 fifteen | 16 sixteen | 17 seventeen |
| 18 eighteen | 19 nineteen | 20 twenty | 21 twenty-one | 22 twenty-two | 23 twenty-three |
| 24 twenty-four | 25 twenty-five | 26 twenty-six | 27 twenty-seven | 28 twenty-eight | 29 twenty-nine |
| 30 thirty | 40 forty | 50 fifty | 60 sixty | 70 seventy | |

## 4  Complete the gaps with the correct numbers.

a) six + _____ = 11

b) _____ + ten = 50

c) _____ + 50 = seventy

d) ten + 19 = _____

e) twenty-four + 24 = _____

f) 20 + _____ = thirty-three

g) _____ + twenty = 30

twenty-three  23

# Now, We Know!

**1** Read and circle *a* or *an*.

a)

a / an girl

b)

a / an dog

c)

a / an elephant

d)

a / an bee

e)

a / an apple

f)

a / an cat

**2** In pairs, write the number sequence.

a) 8 .............. 24 .............. .............. 48

b) .............. 14   21 .............. .............. 42

c) 4   8   12 .............. .............. ..............

d) .............. .............. 15   20   25 ..............

e) .............. .............. 6   9 .............. ..............

**3** Search the words and rewrite the sentences.

a) It is a 🐝 .

b) It is a 🐞 .

c) The 🌿 is green.

d) The 🌷 are red.

e) My 🌸 is beautiful!

f) It is a 🌼 .

g) The 🌼 are yellow and white.

h) The 🦋 is red and blue.

| M | B | V | L | A | D | Y | B | U | G | M | O | P | L |
|---|---|---|---|---|---|---|---|---|---|---|---|---|---|
| R | E | T | Y | C | Q | I | U | B | L | A | P | O | K |
| A | E | Y | T | X | T | U | T | P | E | Y | S | L | J |
| S | T | U | H | Y | S | F | T | Y | D | D | F | Y | D |
| D | U | A | G | A | R | D | E | N | W | S | T | K | A |
| C | I | X | R | U | A | F | R | K | E | A | W | L | I |
| V | K | Z | A | I | S | G | F | L | O | W | E | R | S |
| B | J | U | S | X | K | H | L | A | I | Q | Z | M | Y |
| N | O | P | S | N | O | L | Y | C | R | O | S | E | S |

twenty-five **25**

# Let's Practice!

**1** Listen and match the colors.

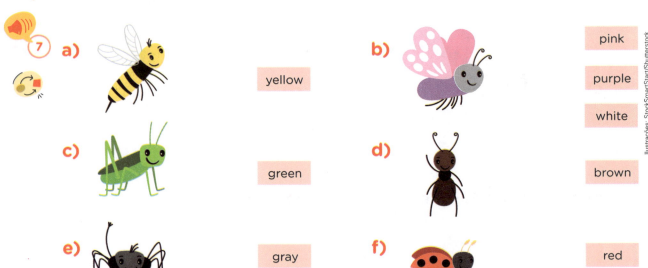

**2** Color the picture and complete the sentence writing the colors.

| 1 - red | 2 - yellow | 3 - blue | 4 - pink | 5 - green |
| 6 - brown | 7 - gray | 8 - purple | 9 - orange |

The sky is _____ , the butterfly is _____ and _____ , the tree is _____ and _____ .

## 3 Listen and make an X.

a)  ☐    ☐

b)  ☐    ☐

c)  ☐    ☐

d)  ☐    ☐

e)  ☐    ☐

f)  ☐    ☐

g)  ☐    ☐

**4** Read the text quickly and make an **X**.

**a)** What is this text about?  ☐ Tourism.  ☐ Food.

**b)** This text is a  ☐ cartoon.  ☐ flyer.

**5** Now, read the text again and do the activity below.

## Visit Inhotim Park!

Visit the largest open air museum in the world!

Inhotim is a museum complex. It gathers more than 500 pieces of contemporary works of art and sculptures in galleries, pavilions and open air.

Come and stroll in our gardens, visit our Botanical Garden designed by Burle Marx.

### Admission Tickets

Tuesday, Thursday, Friday, Saturday, Sunday and Holidays
**Adults:** R$ 44,00 (full price)
**Kids:** under 5 are free of charge / **Kids:** 6 to 12 pay R$ 22,00 (half-entry price)
**Elderly people:** (over 60) pay R$ 22,00 (half-entry price)
**Wednesdays:** free entrance (except holidays)
Closed on Mondays.
**Payment:** in cash or by credit card
**Buy your ticket to visit Inhotim Park at:** http://inhotim.org.br
Rua B, 20, Inhotim – 35460-000 – Brumadinho, MG – Brazil
+55 31 35719700

Write **YES** or **NO**.

**a)** Inhotim is in Rio de Janeiro. _____

**b)** There is a discount for elderly people and children. _____

**c)** Inhotim Park is closed on Mondays. _____

**d)** Payment is in cash only. _____

**6** Complete the information about the Inhotim Park.

a) Telephone number: ................................................................

b) Address: ................................................................
................................................................

**7** Talk to a classmate and answer.

a) Would you like to visit the Inhotim Park? Why?

b) Do you think it is important to visit this kind of museum? Why?

## Let's Sing!

**What a Beautiful Garden!**

Garden, garden, garden!
What a magical place!
Many colored flowers.
And beautiful trees!

Garden, garden, garden!
What an amazing place!
Many curious bugs…
A great nature's feast!

WHAT A BEAUTIFUL GARDEN!

## TALKING ABOUT...

### A Garden in a Plastic Bottle

- What do these pictures represent?
- Do you know someone that has a garden like this at home, at school or in your neighborhood?

**1** Read the words in the word cloud. Then make a glossary.

**2** Let's create a vegetable garden using plastic bottles.

### Let's Learn!
- Verb to be (affirmative, interrogative and short answers)
- What do you have for...? (meals)
- Breakfast food
- Days of the week
- Daily routines
- Telling the time

## LESSON 3 — WHAT'S FOR BREAKFAST?

### Listen and say

## Key Words

**1** Listen, number and say.

| water | toast | cereal | yogurt |

# Language Time

| Verb to be – affirmative | Short form |
|---|---|
| I am | I'm |
| You are | You're |
| He is/She is/It is | He's/She's/It's |
| We are | We're |
| You are | You're |
| They are | They're |
| I am hungry. | I'm hungry. |
| She is beautiful. | She's beautiful. |
| We are at home. | We're at home. |

**1**  Rewrite the sentences using the short form of *to be*.

**a)** I am Tom.

..................................................................................

**b)** He is my friend Daniel.

..................................................................................

**c)** And she is my sister Lily.

..................................................................................

**d)** We are at home.

..................................................................................

**e)** They are my family.

..................................................................................

**2** Circle the words and complete the chart below.

PIZZACHICKENHOT DOGSALADHAMBURGERFISHFRIESFRUIT

| Healthy food | Junk food |
|---|---|
|  |  |
|  |  |
|  |  |
|  |  |

**3** Write the days of the week in order. What day is today? Today is...

Wednesday   Sunday   Saturday   Thursday
Monday   Tuesday   Friday

a) Sunday

b) ..........................

c) ..........................

d) ..........................

e) ..........................

f) ..........................

g) ..........................

**To learn more**

In Brazil and many other countries, the week starts on Monday, but in the United States and Canada, the first day of the week is Sunday.

thirty-seven 37

## Now, We Know!

**1** Listen and complete the chart.

| Snacks for school chart ||
|---|---|
| Days of the week | Healthy snacks for school |
| Monday | |
| Tuesday | |
| Wednesday | |
| Thursday | |
| Friday | |

**2** Read the dialogs and match them to the pictures.

**a)** **A:** Mike, what's for breakfast today?
**B:** Orange juice, cookies and milk.

**b)** **A:** Millie, what's for lunch today?
**B:** French fries, chicken and salad.

**c)** **A:** John, what's for dinner today?
**B:** Spaghetti and apple pie.

**3** Complete with *am*, *is* or *are*.

a) I _____ in the kitchen with Tom and Daniel.

b) Jack _____ in the school library. He _____ happy.

c) Daniel and his father _____ playing basketball. They _____ in the backyard.

d) The students _____ in the Art class. They _____ drawing and painting.

e) The man _____ in the kitchen. He _____ hungry.

# Let's Practice!

**1** Read, circle and make an **X**.

| Are you healthy? | | | |
|---|---|---|---|
|  |  |  |  |
| Hello, I'm Lynn. I have sausages and eggs for breakfast every day. | Hi, I'm Annie. I have a hamburger and French fries for lunch. | Hi, I'm Marco. I have fruit salad and milk for snack. | Hello, I'm Steve. I have chicken, salad and French fries for dinner. |

|  | Lynn | Annie | Marco | Steve |
|---|---|---|---|---|
| eggs |  |  |  |  |
| French fries |  |  |  |  |
| milk |  |  |  |  |
| chicken salad |  |  |  |  |
| hamburger |  |  |  |  |
| sausages |  |  |  |  |
| fruit salad |  |  |  |  |

**2** Listen to the dialog and act out.

**3** Now write about what you have for breakfast, lunch and dinner.

.................................................................................................................................................

.................................................................................................................................................

.................................................................................................................................................

**4** Read the questions and check your preferences. Then talk to a classmate.

**a)** Do you usually go to restaurants or fast food places?

**b)** What do you prefer to eat: junk food or healthy food?

**c)** Check your food and drink preferences.

☐ sandwiches  ☐ chicken  ☐ juice

☐ pizza  ☐ French fries  ☐ ice cream

☐ salad  ☐ soda  ☐ pasta

**5** Read, stick and create a menu.

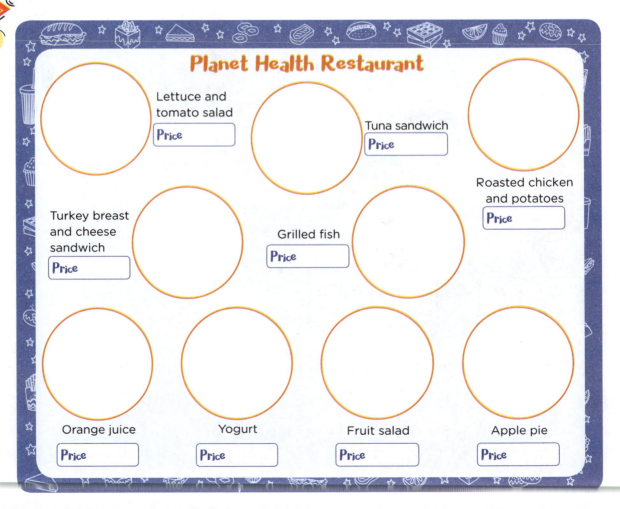

### Planet Health Restaurant

- Lettuce and tomato salad — Price
- Tuna sandwich — Price
- Turkey breast and cheese sandwich — Price
- Grilled fish — Price
- Roasted chicken and potatoes — Price
- Orange juice — Price
- Yogurt — Price
- Fruit salad — Price
- Apple pie — Price

## 6 Read and circle YES or NO.

a) Planet Health is a junk food restaurant.   YES / NO

b) Planet Health has fruit salad on their menu.   YES / NO

c) Planet Health has hot dogs on the menu.   YES / NO

### Let's Sing!

**Breakfast**

I like breakfast.
I eat all the best.
Yogurt and fruit,
they really taste good.
So good, so good,
so good, yeah!

I like breakfast.
I eat all the best.
Fruit cake,
they really taste great
So great, so great,
so great, yeah!

## LESSON 4: IT'S TIME TO GO!

### Listen and say

### Key Words

**1** Look, listen and say.

go to sleep • study • play • have lunch

have breakfast | go to school | wake up | eat

# Language Time

**1** Read the chart and say.

| Verb to be – affirmative | Verb to be – interrogative |
|---|---|
| I **am** a student. | **Am** I a student? |
| You **are** a student. | **Are** you a student? |
| He/She **is** a student. | **Is** he/she a student? |
| It **is** a bird. | **Is** it a bird? |
| We **are** students. | **Are** we students? |
| You **are** students. | **Are** you students? |
| They **are** students. | **Are** they students? |

**2** Rewrite the sentences in the interrogative form.

a) Hamburger is junk food.

..................................................................

b) Sheila is hungry.

..................................................................

c) Oatmeal cookies are healthy food.

..................................................................

d) They are at the restaurant.

..................................................................

e) He is from Brazil.

**3** Read the chart and complete the questions.

| Verb to be – Short answers |
|---|
| Are you a teacher? |
| **Yes, I am. / No, I'm not.** |
| Am I at Class 4? |
| **Yes, you are. / No, you aren't.** |

| Is he/she at school? | Is it a bird? |
|---|---|
| **Yes, he/she is. / No, he/she isn't.** | **Yes, it is. / No, it isn't.** |

| Are we at Class B? |
|---|
| **Yes, you are. / No, you aren't.** |
| Are you good in Math? |
| **Yes, we are. / No, we aren't.** |
| Are they in Canada? |
| **Yes, they are. / No, they aren't.** |

a) _____ Charlie?

Yes, he is.

b) _____ Patty?

Yes, she is.

c) _____ a cat?

No, it isn't.

d) _____ best friends?

Yes, they are.

**4** Listen and say the time.

What time is it?

IT'S 7 O'CLOCK!

IT'S 7:30 A.M.!

## Now, We Know!

**1** Read the text and complete the sentences below with the time.

Hi! My name is Amy Taylor. I am 10 years old and this is my daily routine. I wake up at 6:30 a.m. on weekdays. I have breakfast at 7 o'clock with my mom and my brother and go to school. I have lunch at 12:30 p.m. I usually eat rice, beans, chicken and salad. After lunch, I rest for an hour, then I do my homework. At 4 o'clock I play with my friends. I usually have dinner with my family at 7:30 p.m. After dinner, I watch cartoons on TV and go to sleep at 10 o'clock.

**a)** Amy wakes up at _____.

**b)** She has breakfast at _____.

**c)** She has lunch at _____.

**d)** Amy plays with her friends at _____.

**e)** Amy has dinner with her family at _____.

**f)** She goes to sleep at _____ o'clock.

**2** Read and write the answers about yourself.

It's Sunday! What time do you...?

| wake up | have breakfast | have lunch | play with friends | have dinner | go to sleep |
|---|---|---|---|---|---|
|  |  |  |  |  |  |

48 forty-eight

**3** Choose the words from the box to complete Julie's routine.

> do  go  study  lunch  dinner
> wake  take  have  sleep

Hi. My name is Julie Adams. I am 11 years old and this is my daily routine. Every day I _____ up at 6 o'clock. Then I _____ breakfast and _____ to school. I take the school bus at 7 o'clock.

At 1 o'clock I have _____ with my family and at 3:30 p.m. I _____ and _____ my homework. On Tuesdays and Thursdays, I _____ piano lessons at 4:30 p.m.

At 7:30 p.m. I have _____ and at 10 o'clock I go to _____ .

**4** Write about your daily routine. Then talk to a classmate.

...................................................................................................................

...................................................................................................................

...................................................................................................................

...................................................................................................................

...................................................................................................................

forty-nine **49**

# Let's Practice!

**1** Look at the pictures and draw the clock hands.

**2** Check the correct alternative to the questions.

a) ☐ What time it is?   ☐ What time is it?
It's seven o'clock.

b) ☐ Are you hungry?   ☐ You are hungry?
No, I am not.

c) ☐ You are thirsty?   ☐ Are you thirsty?
Yes, I am.

**3** Read and complete the dialog using the words from the box.

| I'm not   she isn't   they are   he isn't   Is your |

**Charlie:** Hello!

**Grandpa:** Hello, Charlie! It's grandpa here. Is your father home?

**Charlie:** No, _____, grandpa.

**Grandpa:** _____ mother there?

**Charlie:** No, _____.

**Grandpa:** Are they out shopping?

**Charlie:** Yes, _____.

**Grandpa:** Are you home alone, Charlie?

**Charlie:** No, _____ alone. My dog is here with me.

**Grandpa:** Bye, Charlie. Take care!

**Charlie:** Bye, grandpa.

**4** Talk to your classmates. How do you organize your schedule?

**5** Read Tim and Pamela's schedule and stick.

**A busy day!**

Tim and Pamela are very busy on Fridays. They usually wake up at 7 o'clock in the morning.

They have breakfast at 7:30 a.m. and they go to school at 8 o'clock. At 1 o'clock they have lunch at home. Then, they rest for an hour and do homework at 2 o'clock. At 4:30 p.m. they usually play with their friends. At 7 o'clock they have dinner with their family. Then they watch TV or play video game and finally it's time to sleep. It's 9:30 p.m.!

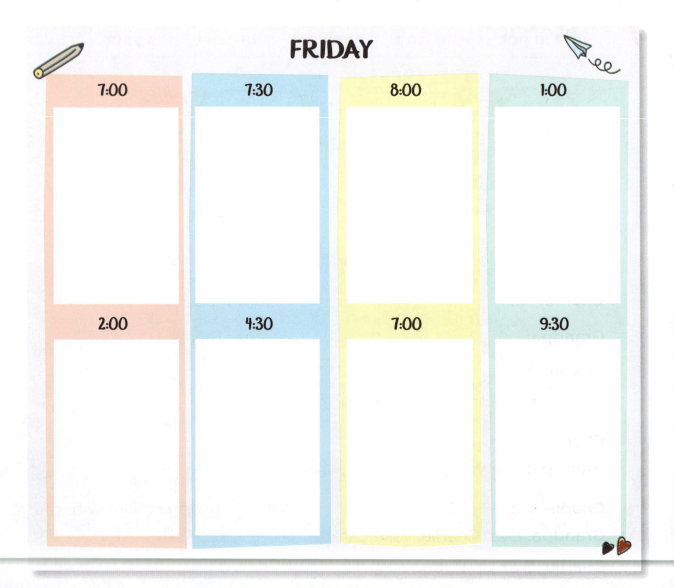

**6** It's Monday. Write your own schedule.

| 7:00 | 7:30 | 8:00 | 12:00 |
|------|------|------|-------|
|      |      |      |       |
| 1:30 | 4:30 | 7:00 | 9:30  |
|      |      |      |       |

## Let's Sing!

**Go… Fast, Slow!**

Every day the hours go

Sometimes fast,

And sometimes slow.

Tell me what the clock shows

It's seven o'clock,

It's time to go.

Tell me what the clock shows

It's twelve o'clock,

It's time for lunch.

Tell me what the clock shows

It's ten at night,

It's time to sleep.

And have a good night

At least!

# IT'S YOUR TURN!

## Let's Make a Meals Record Chart!

 Follow the steps below.

### YOU NEED:

- A4 sheets of paper

- Scissors

- Colored markers

- Whiteboard markers

- Transparent adhesive paper

- Cardboard paper

1) Draw your chart in a piece of paper.

2) Use your creativity to decorate your chart.

3) Glue your chart to the cardboard paper.

4) Cover it with transparent adhesive paper.

5) Hang the meals chart on the fridge door in your house.

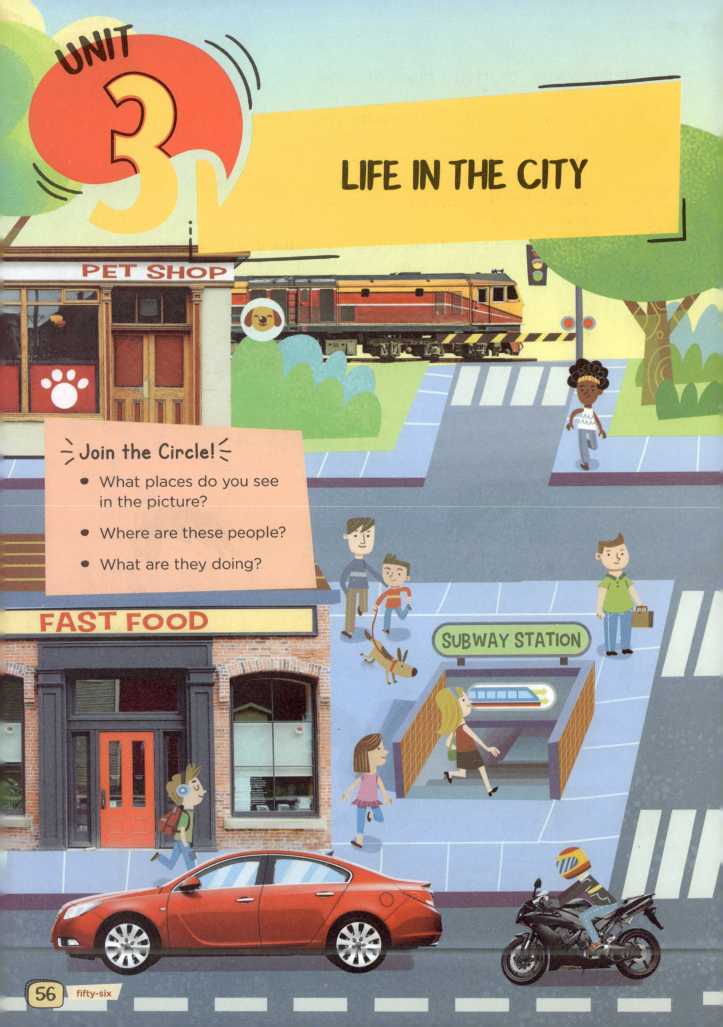

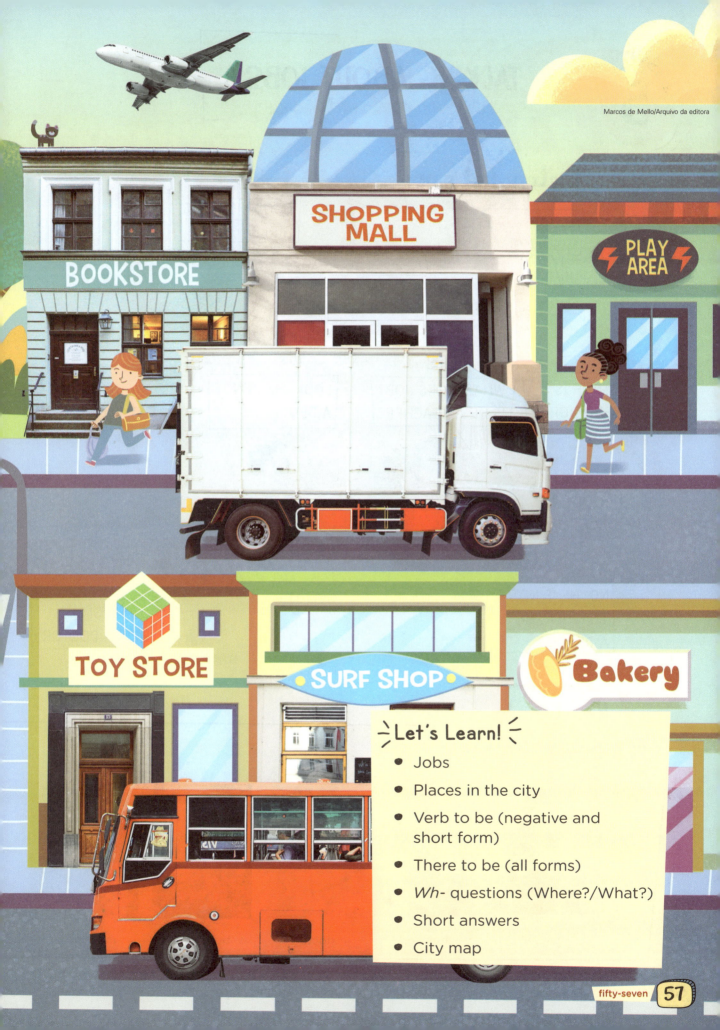

# LESSON 5
# TALKING ABOUT JOBS

## Key Words

**1** Look, listen and say.

lawyer     engineer     doctor     bus driver     mechanic

# Language Time

**1** Read the chart about *Wh-* questions.

| WH- QUESTIONS | Functions | Examples |
|---|---|---|
| What | ask for information about something | **What** is her job? She is an engineer. |
| Where | ask about places or positions | **Where** is her office? It is four blocks from here. |

**2** Look at the pictures, read and answer.

**a)** Gregory is a doctor. Is he at the hospital now? Yes, he is. Where is the hospital? It is five blocks from here.

**b)** Lucy is a baker. Is she at the bakery now? Yes, she is. Where is the bakery? It is two blocks from here.

**c)** Sarah is a teacher. Is she at school now? Yes, she is. Where is the school? It is six blocks from here.

I. **Who** is a doctor? ........................

II. **What** is Lucy's job? ........................

III. **Where** is Gregory's work? ........................

IV. **What** is Sarah's job? ........................

V. **Where** is the bakery? ........................

**3** Read the chart with the negative form of verb to be.

| Verb to be – negative | Short form |
|---|---|
| I am not | I'm not |
| You are not | You aren't |
| He/She/It is not | He/She/It isn't |
| We are not | We aren't |
| You are not | You aren't |
| They are not | They aren't |

is not = isn't / are not = aren't

**4** Rewrite the sentences in the negative form.

a) We are teachers.

...................................................................................

b) They are lawyers.

...................................................................................

c) You are a baker.

...................................................................................

d) She is a dentist.

...................................................................................

e) He is a famous singer.

...................................................................................

f) I am a mechanic.

...................................................................................

# Now, We Know!

**1** Listen and circle.

a)

b)

c)

d)

e)

f)

g)

**2** Listen and act out.

# Let's Practice!

**1** Complete with *am*, *is* or *are*. Unscramble the letters to find what they do.

a) My name ............ Polly Jones. I ............ not a lawyer. I am a ............................ (rehcaet).

b) This ............ my brother Bill. He ............ not a bus driver. He is an ................................ (reengine).

c) This ............ my sister Helen. She ............ not a dentist. She is a ................................ (rotcod).

d) This ............ my mother Sue and this ............ my father Tom. They ................................ (srekah).

**2** Rewrite the sentences in the interrogative form and answer.

a) They are teachers. (yes)

...................................................................................................................

b) She is a lawyer. (no)

...................................................................................................................

c) You are a bus driver. (yes)

...................................................................................................................

d) She is a dentist. (no)

...................................................................................................................

e) He is a mechanic. (yes)

...................................................................................................................

**3** Look at the picture and complete the text with the words from the box.

| neighbor | isn't | doctor | is | tall | he |

**My neighbor Meghan**

That young lady is my ............................................... .

She ............................................... Meghan Franklin.

Ms. Franklin ............................................... a dentist.

She is a ............................................... .

She isn't ............................................... . She is short.

Her father is Mr. Franklin.

............................................... is a mechanic.

Look over there! He is that ............................................... man.

**4** Which ones are new professions and occupations? Make an **X**.

- [x] dentist
- [ ] teacher
- [ ] climate change specialist
- [ ] drone operator
- [ ] global warm specialist
- [ ] agricultural and food scientist

**5** Read the text and complete.

**Greta Thunberg, schoolgirl climate change warrior**

**Birth date:** January 3, 2003.

**Birth name:** Greta Tintin Eleonora Ernman Thunberg

**Parents:** Malena Ernman, Svante Thunberg

**Occupation:** student, environmental activist

**Birth place:** Stockholm, Sweden

• Greta Thunberg is a schoolgirl who has a special mission: she is a climate change activist.

Greta ................... a ................................... and an ............................................................. . She was born on ........................................................, 2003. She is from ..............................................., Sweden. Her parents .................. Malena and Svante.

## Let's Sing!

**Jobs**

Working as a lawyer
My work is a law.
Now the day is over,
I come home to read a lot.

Working as a doctor
I'm always alert.
Now the day is over,
I hope I can rest.

Working as a teacher
I stay with children and teens.
Now the day is over,
And I'm still correcting things.

**1** Choose the correct sentence for each speech bubble and write.

> My neighbor is a doctor.   She is a teacher, Tom.
> No, he is a dentist.   I am a mechanic.

# AROUND THE CITY

## Listen and say

HEY, KIDS! LET'S GO TO THE NEW MALL.

GOOD IDEA! WHERE IS THE NEW MALL?

IT IS FIVE BLOCKS FROM HERE.

HOW CAN WE GET THERE?

## Key Words

**1** Look, listen and say.

pet shop

toy store

surf shop

fast food place

play area

bookstore

# Language Time

| There to be |||
|---|---|---|
| **Affirmative** | **Interrogative** | **Negative** |
| **There is** a shopping mall in the city. | **Is there** a shopping mall in the city? | **There isn't** a shopping mall in the city. |
| **There are** two toy stores in the city. | **Are there** two toy stores in the city? | **There aren't** two toy stores in the city. |

| Short answers ||
|---|---|
| Is there a bus in the picture?<br>**Yes, there is.** / **No, there isn't.** | Are there two scooters in the picture?<br>**Yes, there are.** / **No, there aren't.** |

**1** Count and complete the sentences with **there is** or **there are**.

In this picture _____ two planes in the sky.

_____ one bus. _____ four cars.

_____ two bikes. _____ three motorcycles. _____ one man riding a scooter.

**2**   In pairs, look at the map and match questions and answers.

a) Is there a mall in the map, Daniel? Where is it?

☐ No, there isn't.

b) Is there a subway station in the map, Lily? Where is it?

☐ Yes, there is. It's four blocks from here.

c) Is there a train station in the map, Daniel?

☐ Yes, there is. It's two blocks from here.

d) Is there a bookstore in the map, Lily? Where is it?

☐ Yes, there is. It's three blocks from here.

## Now, We Know!

**1** Listen and write **YES** or **NO**.

**2** Where can you find these items?

a)

In a ............................................

b)

In a ............................................

c)

In a ............................................

d)

In a ............................................

# To learn more

In the United States and Canada, the commercial centers full of stores and restaurants are called *mall*, an abbreviation for *shopping mall*, and not *shopping* as Brazilians do.

In the United Kingdom, people usually say *shopping center*, but never say "shopping" only as we do in Brazil.

**3** Match the columns.

a) Bookstore — toys and games

b) Fast food place — books, CDs, DVDs

c) Play area — animals, food, accessories

d) Pet shop — juices, sandwiches and ice creams

e) Surf shop — electronic and interactive games

f) Toy store — surfboards, surf equipment, clothes

**4** Listen, number and say.

a) b) c) d)

e) f) g) h)

seventy-three 73

# Let's Practice!

**1** How can we help the environment? Read and make an **X**.

☐ Ride a bike to work.                    ☐ Take the bus.

☐ Drive a big car.                        ☐ Carpool when possible.

☐ Have an electric car.                   ☐ Drive an economic car.

☐ Use a gas fuel car.

**2** Read and write **T** (true) or **F** (false).

### Help the Environment

To reduce air pollution, we need fewer cars on the streets.

It is a good idea to make journeys by bike, by bus or on foot.

We can walk to school, ride a bike in short distances or travel by bus. Let's help the environment and make our life better.

Based on: <https://www.letsride.co.uk/article/bike-love/10-reasons-why-cycling-is-better-than-driving>. Accessed on: October 30, 2019.

**a)** We need fewer cars on the streets to reduce air pollution. ☐

**b)** We can reduce air pollution using cars. ☐

**c)** We can walk to school, ride a bike or travel by bus to help the environment. ☐

**d)** We can make our life better. ☐

**3** Read and answer.

 **a)** How do you go to school?

........................................................................................

**b)** How does your father or mother go to work?

........................................................................................

**c)** What type of transport does your family use most? Why?

........................................................................................

**4** Read, listen and write the name of the place.

 **a)** ........................................................................................

 **b)** ........................................................................................

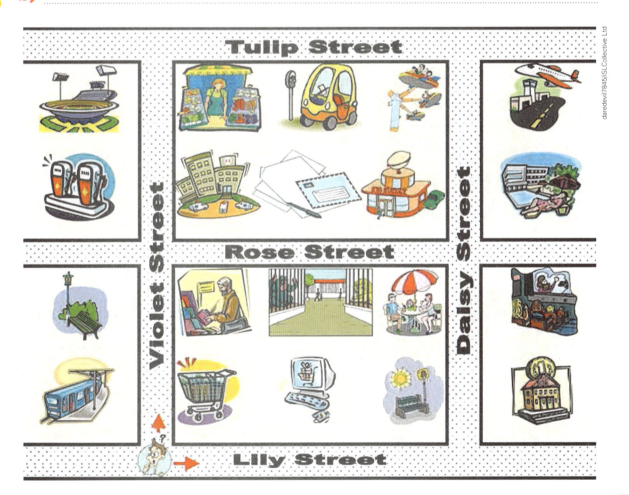

## 5 Read and answer.

**a)** Is there a shopping mall near your school?

☐ Yes, there is. ☐ No, there isn't.

**b)** Is there a play area near your house?

☐ Yes, there is. ☐ No, there isn't.

**c)** Are there bus stops around this school?

☐ Yes, there are. ☐ No, there aren't.

**d)** Are there bookstores near your house?

☐ Yes, there are. ☐ No, there aren't.

## 6 Listen and complete.

**a)**

**A:** Let's go to the _____.
**B:** Where is the _____?
**A:** It is _____ from here.
**B:** How can we get there?
**A:** On _____.

**b)**

**A:** Let's go to the _____.
**B:** Where is the _____?
**A:** It is _____ from here.
**B:** How can we get there?
**A:** By _____.

## Let's Sing!

**1** Listen and order the lyrics. Write **A**, **B**, **C** in the parentheses.

**The Wheels on the Bus**

☐ The people on the bus go up and down,
Up and down, up and down,
The people on the bus go up and down,
All through the town.

☐ The horn on the bus goes toot, toot, toot…
The money in the box goes ching, ching, ching…
The wiper on the glass goes swish, swish, swish…
The driver on the bus says "Move on back".

☐ The wheels on the bus go round and round,
Round and round, round and round.
The wheels on the bus go round and round,
All through the town.

**2** Find 5 means of transportation in the word search.

- Write them here.

1. ........................................
2. ........................................
3. ........................................
4. ........................................
5. ........................................

seventy-seven 77

## The Importance of Each Profession

 • Look at the pictures and think about the future of some jobs.

**1** Match the pictures and the descriptions.

☐ A person employed to cart away household garbage.

☐ A person who can operate a drone.

☐ A qualified practitioner of medicine; a physician.

☐ A person who delivers or collects letters and parcels.

☐ A person whose job is to extinguish fires.

☐ A person who teaches, especially in schools.

☐ A person who designs, builds, or maintains engines, machines, or public works.

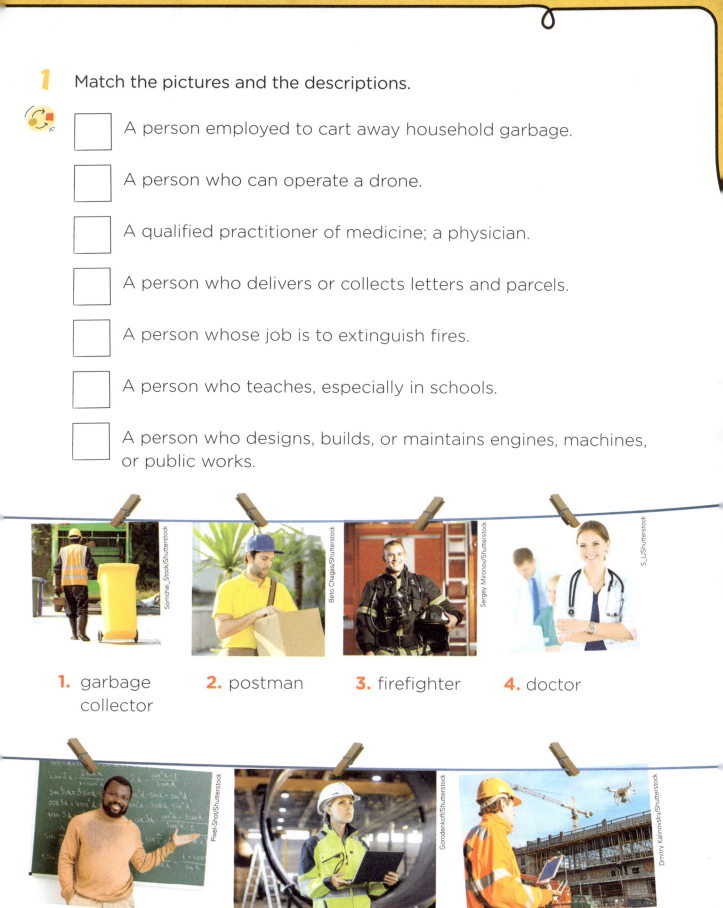

1. garbage collector
2. postman
3. firefighter
4. doctor
5. teacher
6. engineer
7. drone pilot

seventy-nine **79**

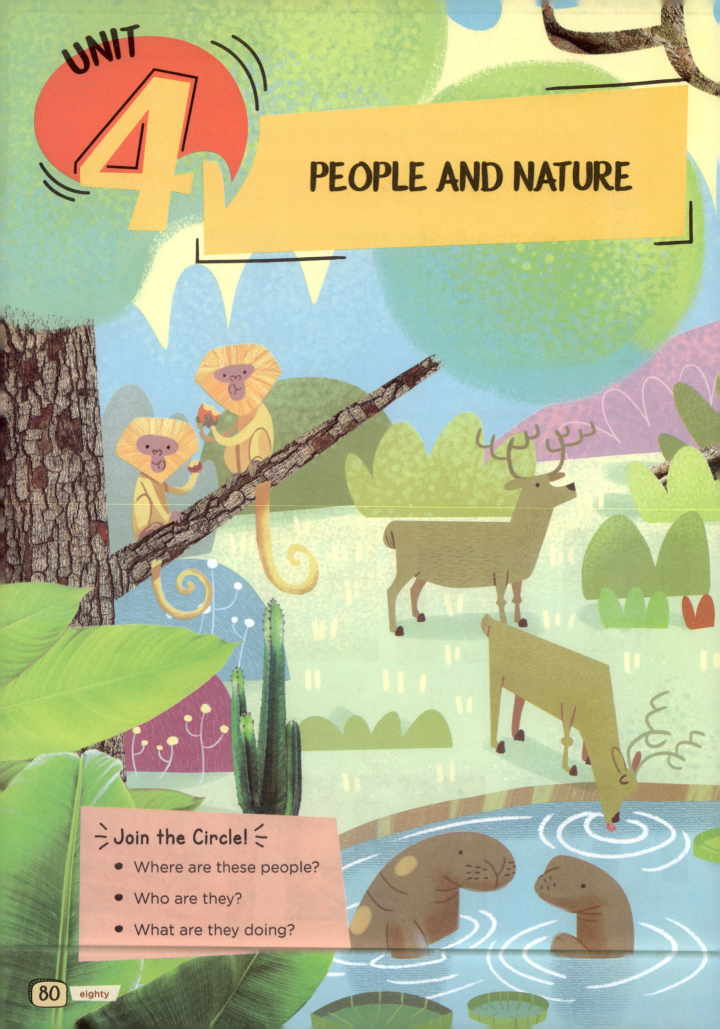

Let's Learn!
- Animals
- Clothes and accessories
- Months of the year
- There to be
- How many...?
- Why?/Because...

# LESSON 7
# SAVE THE ANIMALS!

## Listen and say

## Key Words

**1** Look, listen and say.

blue macaw

manatee

giant panda bear

golden lion tamarin

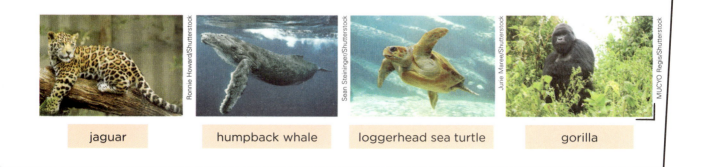

jaguar humpback whale loggerhead sea turtle gorilla

# Language Time

| | There to be ||
|---|---|---|
| | Singular form | Plural form |
| **Affirmative** | There is a giant panda bear on TV now. | There are five children watching TV at Lily's house. |
| **Negative** | There isn't (is not) a giant panda bear on TV now. | There aren't (are not) five children watching TV at Lily's house. |
| **Interrogative** | Is there a giant panda bear on TV now? | Are there five children watching TV at Lily's house? |
| **Short answers** | Yes, there is.<br>No, there isn't (is not). | Yes, there are.<br>No, there aren't (are not). |

**1**  Look at the pictures and answer **T** (true) or **F** (false). Rewrite the false ones.

**a)** There is a gorilla under the tree. ☐

..................................................................................................

**b)** There is a jaguar in the jungle. ☐

..................................................................................................

**c)** There is a humpback whale swimming in the ocean. ☐

..................................................................................................

**d)** There are three manatees in the picture. ☐

..................................................................................................

**e)** There are two panda bears in the bamboo forest. ☐

..................................................................................................

**2** How many animals? Listen and stick.

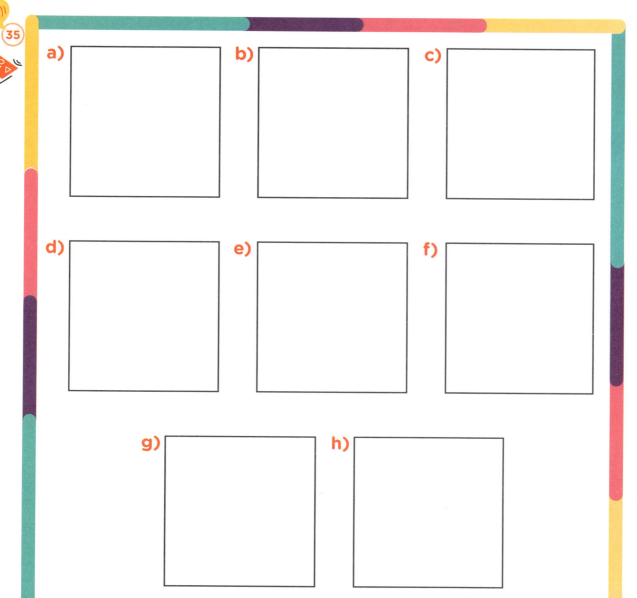

## To learn more

The Brazilian non-profit organization owned by the Chico Mendes Institute for Biodiversity Conservation created the Projeto TAMAR in 1980. Since the 1970s sea turtles were in the endangered species list due to incidental capture during fishing, killing of female turtles and capture of their laid eggs. Since then, more than 37 million little turtles were returned to the ocean. To read more, access <http://www.tamar.org.br/#>. Accessed on: March 5, 2020.

# Now, We Know!

**1** Listen and make an **X**.

36

a)

Hung Chung Chih/Shutterstock

Pedro Helder Pinheiro/Shutterstock

b)

Aliioss xeii/Shutterstock

Thierry Eidenweil/Shutterstock

c)

Madeline Jewett/Shutterstock

NaturePicsFilms/Shutterstock

d)

meunierd/Shutterstock

Jurgen Vogt/Shutterstock

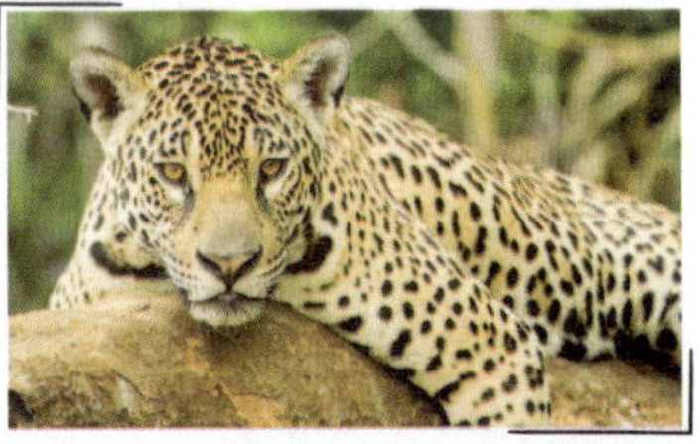

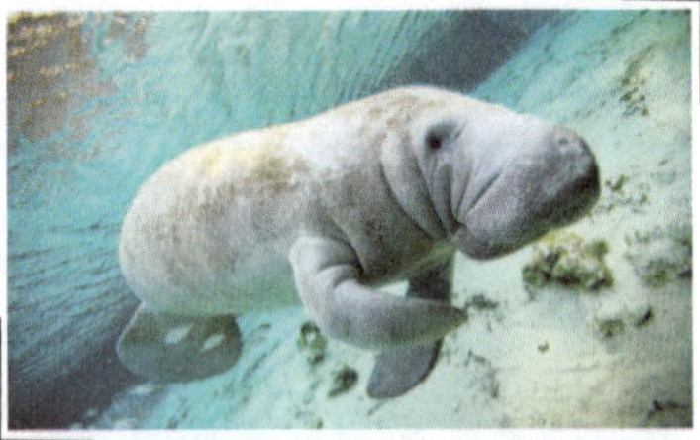

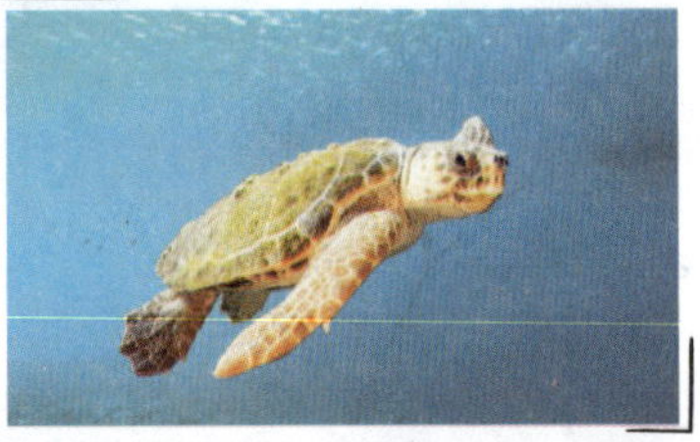

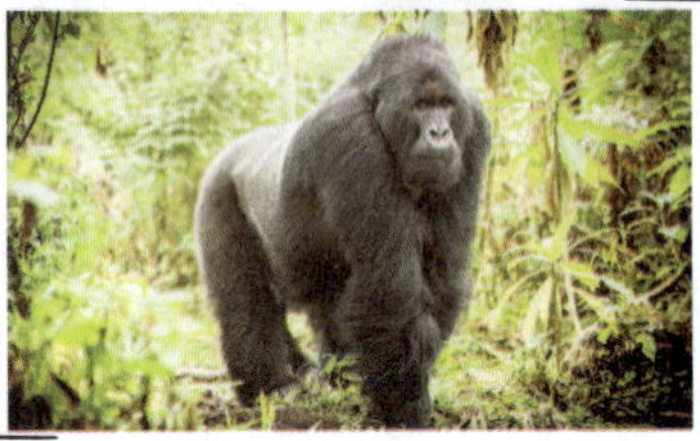

**2** Match the sentences to the pictures from activity 1.

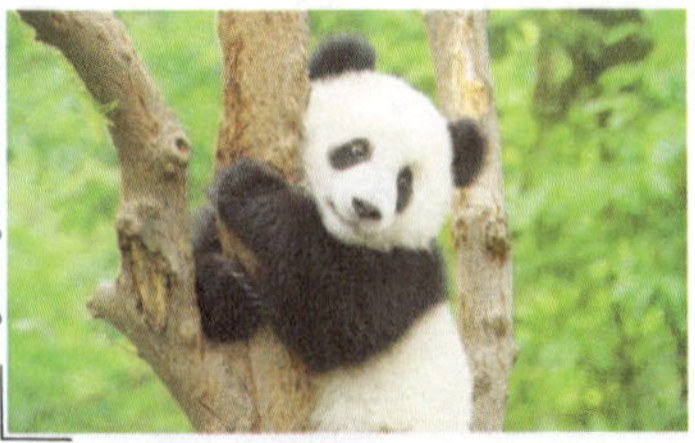

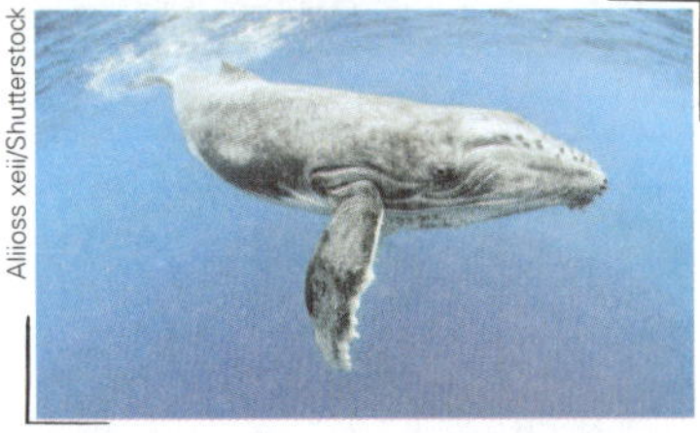

a) The golden lion tamarin is a mammal that lives mostly in Rio de Janeiro, Brazil. Its hair is golden and beautiful.

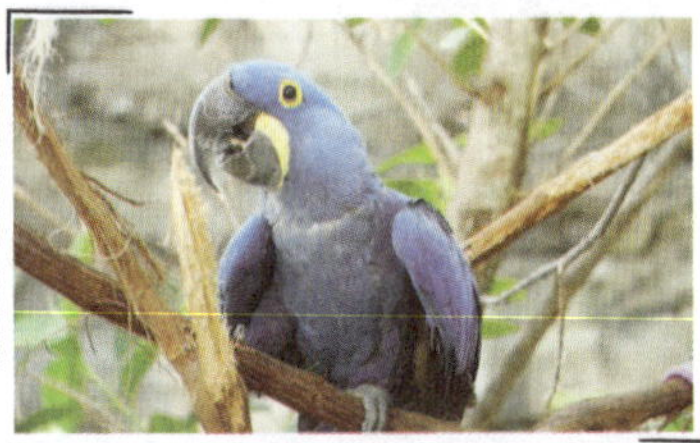

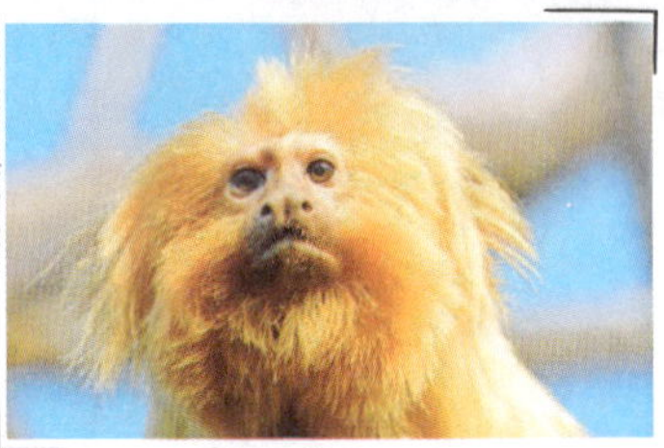

b) The loggerhead sea turtle is in the endangered species list. It lives up to 50 years or more.

c) The giant panda bear is cute. It is black and white and eats mostly bamboo. It lives in the mountains in China.

d) The humpback whale is a big animal. It can be found in oceans around the world.

**3** Look, read and circle the correct answers.

a) There is a manatee in this picture.

Yes, there is.
No, there isn't.

b) There is a boy drawing a whale in this picture.

Yes, there is.
No, there isn't.

c) There are two boys coloring the monster picture.

Yes, there are.
No, there aren't.

d) There is a gorilla in this picture.

Yes, there is.
No, there isn't.

**4** Listen and act out.

**Lily:** Kim, let's do some research on the internet about endangered animals.

**Kim:** Yes! Let's find some interesting facts about the animals!

**Lily:** So, we can write our school report.

**Kim:** We can find websites about every topic we want on the internet.

**Lily:** Let's surf the internet.

**Kim:** OK, Lily!

# Let's Practice!

**1** Complete the crossword puzzle.

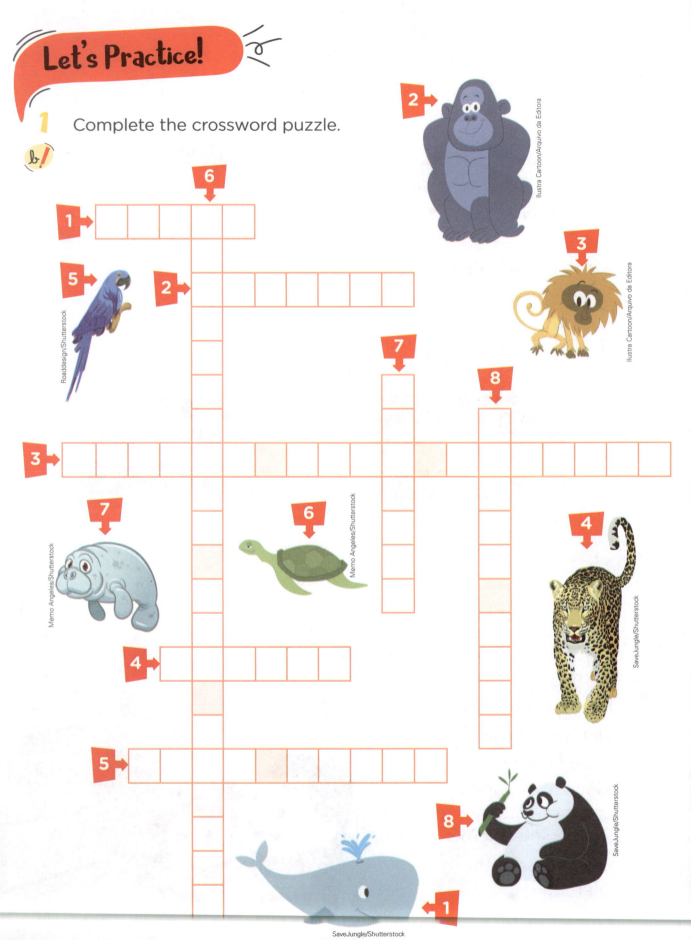

**2** Match the questions to the answers.

a) Is there a beautiful jaguar in the zoo?

b) How many panda bears are in the picture?

c) Are there gorillas in tropical forests?

d) Is there a humpback whale in the ocean?

e) How many blue macaws are there in the tree?

☐ There are five blue macaws in the tree.

☐ Yes, there is a humpback whale in the ocean.

☐ There are four panda bears in the picture.

☐ Yes, there is a beautiful jaguar in the zoo.

☐ Yes, there are gorillas in tropical forests.

**3** In pairs, read the animal riddles and write their names.

| sea turtle | panda bear | blue macaw | whale |

a) I am a reptile. I live in the water and can breathe air. I lay eggs in the sand. I have four legs.

I am a _____.

b) I am a big mammal and I live in the ocean. I can jump very high in the water. I eat lots of fish.

I am a _____.

c) I am a mammal, too. I am black and white. I usually eat bamboo leaves. I live in the bamboo forests in China.

I am a _____.

d) I am a bird. I have blue wings and tail, a black beak and I can fly. I eat nuts.

I am a _____.

**4** Look at the picture in activity 5 and circle the correct answer.

a) Is this animal a mammal?     YES     NO

b) Is its natural habitat the ocean?     YES     NO

**5** Read the text and check the correct answers.

### ANIMAL FACT FILE – THE MARSH DEER

**Popular name:** Marsh deer

**Scientific name:** *Blastocerus dichotomous*

**Life range:** 10 to 30 years

**Weight:** 80 to 150 kilos

**Height:** about 2 meters (adult)

**Habitat:** Pantanal Wetland (Brazil)

**Diet/Eating habits:** aquatic plants and grass

**Marsh deer fun facts:**
Marsh deers are mammals.
Their color is brown in the winter and light brown in the summer.

**Other interesting facts:**
Their gestation lasts 270 days.
A marsh deer young baby is called a fawn.
Listed as *vulnerable* animals by the International Union for the Conservation of Nature an Natural Resources (IUCN)

Based on: <https://thewebsiteofeverything.com/animals/mammals/Artiodactyla/Cervidae/Blastocerus/Blastocerus-dichotomus.html>. Accessed on: Jan. 22, 2020.

a) Marsh deers eat ............ and grass.
☐ fish     ☐ meat     ☐ aquatic plants

b) An adult marsh deer can weight up to ............ kilos.
☐ 200     ☐ 150     ☐ 90

c) Marsh deers are ............ .
☐ fish     ☐ reptiles     ☐ mammals

**6** Choose an animal and write about it in your notebook. Then share with a classmate.

### Let's Sing!

**One Elephant Went Out to Play**

One elephant went out to play,
Out on a spider's web one day,
He had such enormous fun,
He called for another elephant
to come.

Two elephants went out to play,
Out on a spider's web one day,
They had such enormous fun,
They called for another elephant
to come.

Three elephants went out to play,
Out on a spider's web one day,
They had such enormous fun,
They called for another elephant
to come.

**7** Break the code and write the sentence.

| 1 | 2 | 3 | 4 | 5 | 6 | 7 | 8 | 9 | 10 | 11 | 12 |
|---|---|---|---|---|---|---|---|---|----|----|----|
| a | c | e | h | i | l | m | n | p | r  | s  | t  |

| 10 | 3 | 11 | 9 | 3 | 2 | 12 |

| 12 | 4 | 3 |

| 1 | 8 | 5 | 7 | 1 | 6 | 11 |

# LESSON 8: A COOL TRIP!

## Listen and say

## Key Words

**1** Look, listen and say.

dress     skirt     shorts     jeans     T-shirt

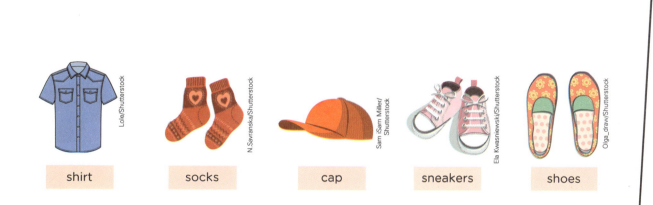

# Language Time

| How many...? | |
|---|---|
| How many months are there in a year? | There are 12 months in a year. |
| How many days are there in a week? | There are 7 days in a week. |
| How many students are there in the classroom? | There are 30 students in the classroom. |

**1** Look at the pictures and make an **X**.

**a)** How many clothes are there on the clothing rack 1?

There are...

☐ two skirts on the clothing rack.

☐ three dresses on the clothing rack.

☐ two jeans on the clothing rack.

☐ one black sweater on the clothing rack.

1

**b)** How many clothes are there on the clothing rack 2?

There are...

☐ four pairs of pants on the clothing rack.

☐ two dresses on the clothing rack.

☐ two T-shirts on the clothing rack.

☐ one green jacket on the clothing rack.

2

**2** Complete the names of the months with vowels.

## The Brazilian Calendar

J___n___ry — Summer School Holidays
F___br___ry — Back to School/Carnival
M___rch — International Women's Day
___pr___l — Easter
M___y — Mother's Day
J___n___ — June Feasts
J___ly — Winter
___g___st — Father's Day
S___pt___mb___r — Spring
___ct___b___r — Children's Day
N___v___mb___r — School Final Tests
D___c___mb___r — Christmas

# Now, We Know!

**1** Listen and make an **X**.

a)

b)

c)

d)

e)

**2** What are they wearing? Write the names of the clothes.

**3** How many pieces of clothes are there?

**a)** There are three pants, ..............................................

..............................................

**1** Listen and make an **X**.

a)

☐ Yes   ☐ No

b)

☐ Yes   ☐ No

c)

☐ Yes   ☐ No

d)

☐ Yes   ☐ No

**2** Listen to the dialog and act out.

**3** Write the seasons of the year using the words from the box. Then match.

fall    spring    summer    winter

a) September, October and November

b) December, January and February

c) March, April and May

d) June, July and August

**4** Complete the sentences with *there is* or *there are*.

a) ............................. three people running.

b) ............................. a woman walking with a baby.

c) ............................. two girls riding a bike.

d) ............................. a boat in the lake.

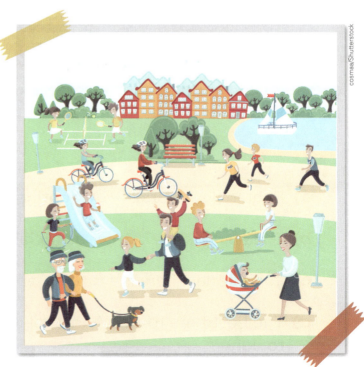

**5** Talk to a classmate about traveling.

**a)** Where do you like to go when you travel?

**b)** How do you find information about the place you want to visit?

**6** Read the travel blog post and circle the correct answers.

**Explore Pantanal!**

For animal watching, you must visit Pantanal in Brazil. The word "pantanal" means wetland areas. Stay in Campo Grande city to visit a big park to see capybaras walking around and different birds. The capybara is cute.

Pantanal is home to an immense variety of wildlife – if you are adventurous, go to a night safari to see caimans at the lake. Go on a jeep drive or boat trip to see monkeys and more exotic birds. I saw many blue macaws and toucan birds too. We also saw marsh deers, giant anteaters, otters, jaguars, etc.

The best time to visit Pantanal is from July to October during the dry season. You must visit Bonito! It is an ecotourism city full of wildlife, waterfalls, caves and crystal-clear rivers.

Visit Pantanal and have a great adventure!

**a)** Pantanal is in **Brazil** / **Argentina**.

**b)** The animals are in their **artificial** / **natural** habitat.

**c)** In Pantanal, there is a **small** / an **immense** variety of wildlife.

**d)** The best time to visit Pantanal is from **July to October** / **May to July**.

**7** Would you like to visit Pantanal? Why (not)?

## 🎵 Let's Sing!

**Ms. Red Bow**

Today Ms. Red Bow
Looks like a rainbow.
Green shoes, violet socks,
Yellow T-shirt and pink skirt.
A red and blue sweater,
And an indigo hat.
This is her way of dressing.
She thinks she couldn't look better!

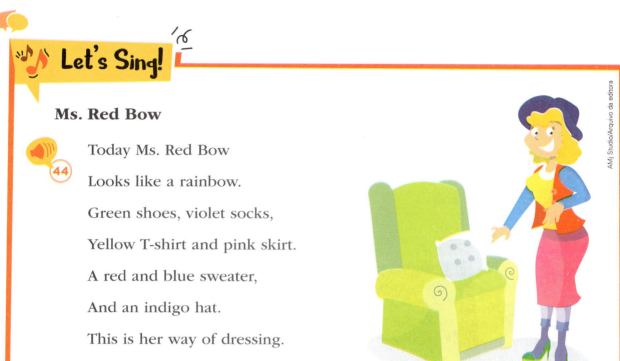

**8** Follow the path and answer the questions. Then draw.

What's this? It's a ..................................... .

| sweater | shorts | skirt | shoes | cap |
| socks | sneakers | dress | T-shirt | jeans |

# IT'S YOUR TURN!

## Let's Make a Pantanal Model!

 In groups, follow the steps below.

### YOU NEED:

- wood sawdust or soil

- green and brown crepe paper (trees) and colored crepe paper (flowers)

- blue cellophane paper (water)

- glue, scissors, barbecue wooden skewers

- a piece of thick cardboard paper

- plastic miniatures of wild animals or colored dough to model animals

1) Cover the cardboard with brown paper, soil or wood sawdust. Use white glue.

2) Draw the lakes and the wetlands. Cut and glue them on the cardboard. Use the cellophane paper to represent the water.

3) Model the animals or use the plastic miniatures to add to the scene. Write the name of the animals on paper labels.

4) Make the trees and bushes with cardboard base or barbecue wooden skewers, cover them with brown and green crepe paper.

5) Then decorate it with some flowers made of colored crepe paper and place the animals on it.

# REVIEW  At Home

**1** Match the sentences to the pictures.

a) I am in the laundry room.

b) It is in the garage.

c) They are in the living room.

d) They are in the bedroom.

e) She is in the backyard.

f) He is in the dining room.

# REVIEW: A Beautiful Garden

**1** Find and circle eight words. Then write them.

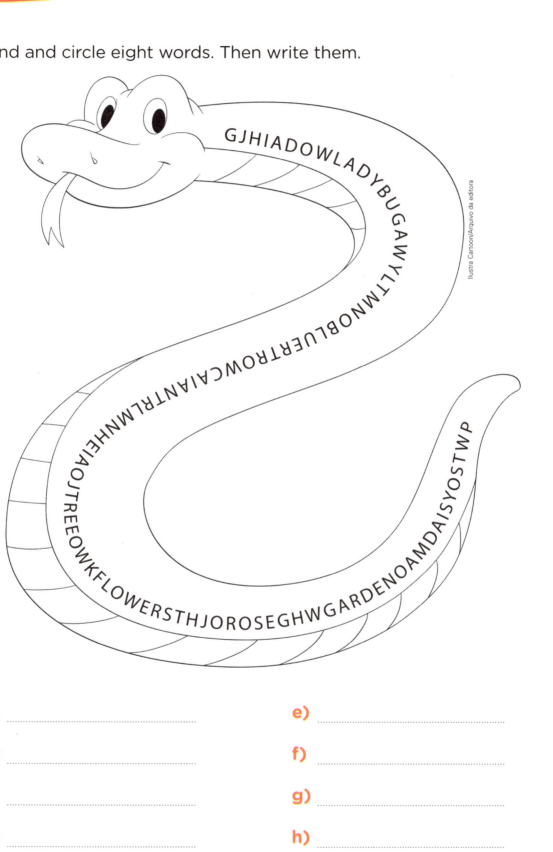

a) ..................................................  e) ..................................................

b) ..................................................  f) ..................................................

c) ..................................................  g) ..................................................

d) ..................................................  h) ..................................................

# REVIEW → What's for Breakfast?

**1** Unscramble the words and match the pictures.

**a)** t r u g o y

....................................................

**b)** l a e r e c

....................................................

**c)** r c F e n s e i f r h

....................................................

**d)** t a s o t

....................................................

**e)** r e w t a

....................................................

**f)** p z a z i

....................................................

# REVIEW ~ It's Time to Go!

**1** Look at the pictures and write.

a)

..................................................

b)

..................................................

c)

..................................................

d)

..................................................

e)

..................................................

f)

..................................................

one hundred and seven 107

# REVIEW → Talking about Jobs

**1**  Choose the correct sentence for each picture.

> Larry is a postman. Susan is a baker.
> Paul and Melina are doctors. Edward is a policeman.
> Lisa is a dentist. Tony is a mechanic.

a)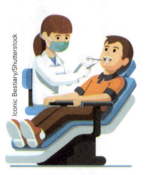

d)

b)

e)

c)

f)

# REVIEW — Around the City

**1** Look at the pictures and name the places.

a)

c)

...........................................

...........................................

b)

d)

...........................................

...........................................

**2** Write questions with *Is there...?* or *Are there...?*. Look at the picture and answer using short answers.

a) ........................................... two dogs by the window in the pet shop? ........................................... .

b) ........................................... two boys in the toy store?
...........................................

c) ........................................... a bird in the pet shop?
...........................................

one hundred and nine 109

# REVIEW: Save the Animals!

**1** How many animals? Count and answer with *there is* or *there are*.

a)

.................................................... humpback whales.

b)

.................................................... blue macaws.

c)

.................................................... manatees.

d)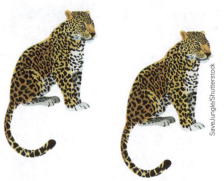

.................................................... jaguars.

e)

.................................................... loggerhead sea turtle.

# REVIEW: A Cool Trip!

**1** Write the missing letters and then match.

a) D [ ] [ ] s [ ]

b) S [ ] i [ ] [ ]

c) S [ ] [ ] [ ] [ ] s

d) S h [ ] [ ] [ ]

e) J [ ] [ ] n [ ]

f) S [ ] c [ ] [ ]

g) T - [ ] [ ] i [ ] [ ]

h) C [ ] p

i) S [ ] a k [ ] [ ] [ ]

j) S [ ] [ ] e [ ]

## LET'S PLAY! At Home

**1** Unscramble the letters and write the parts of the house.

a) hetcnki      kitc**h**en

b) gniidn moor      ................**o**................

c) gnivli oorm      ................**m**

d) moordeb      ........**e**........

e) thoomrab      ........................

**2** Use the clues from activity 1, guess the word and write.

| T | h | i | s |  | i | s |  | m | y |  |  |  |  |  |

112 one hundred and twelve

# LET'S PLAY! A Beautiful Garden

**1** Decode the words and write.

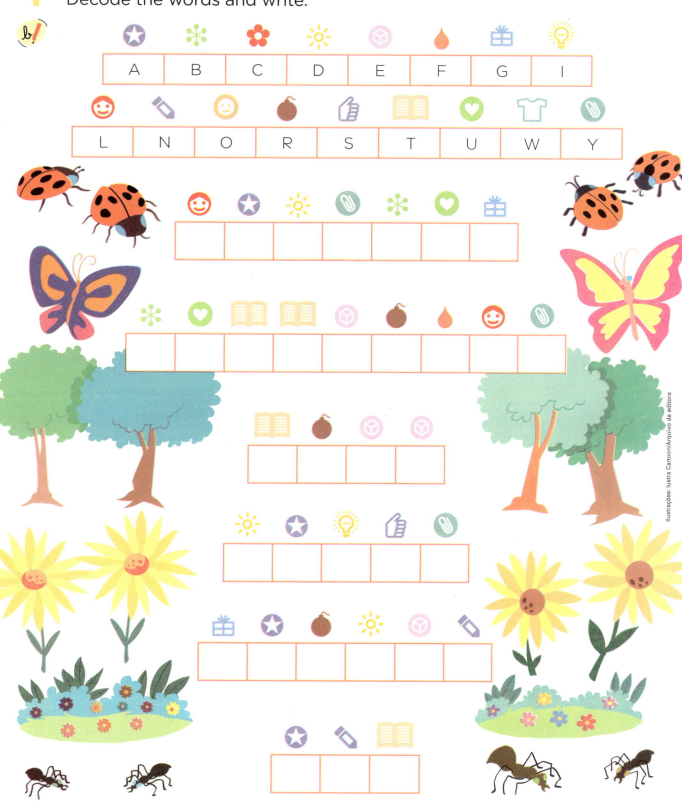

## LET'S PLAY! What's for Breakfast?

**1** Let's color the picture.

1 – light gray
2 – red
3 – purple
4 – gray
5 – black
6 – brown
7 – violet
8 – navy blue
9 – blue
10 – pink
11 – yellow
12 – green

**2** Crossword.

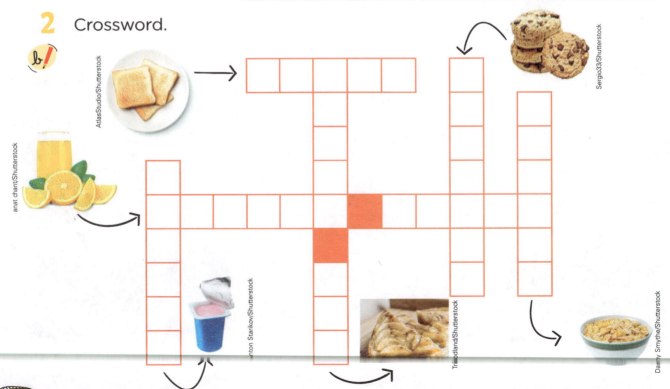

# LET'S PLAY! It's Time to Go!

**1** Use these letters to complete the name of eight means of transportation. Then draw them in the boxes.

| A | B | C | E | I | K | L | M | H |
|---|---|---|---|---|---|---|---|---|
| N | O | R | S | U | T | P | Y | W |

a)

t............................................

b)

m............................................

c)

t............................................

d)

p............................................

e)

c............................................

f)

s............................................

g)

b............................................

h)

s............................................

# LET'S PLAY! Talking about Jobs

**1** Bingo. Choose eight words from the box and write them in the bingo card.

| patient | job | mother | engineer | game |
| bus driver | play | parents | father | baker |
| teacher | neighbor | student | sister | postman |
| dentist | policeman | dog | children | brother |
| | postwoman | mechanic | lawyer | doctor |

### BINGO CARD

| | |
|---|---|
| | |
| | |
| | |
| | |

one hundred and sixteen

## LET'S PLAY! Around the City

**1** Complete the sentences with *there is* or *there are*.

a) ................................................
two cars in the garage.

b) ................................................
a motorcycle in the street.

c) ................................................
two toy boats in my swimming pool.

d) ................................................
a toy plane in the toy store window.

e) ................................................
four tables and three stools in the food court.

one hundred and seventeen 117

# LET'S PLAY! Save the Animals!

**1** Match the pictures to the animal names.

a)   Jaguar

b)   Golden lion tamarin

c)   Humpback whale

d)   Blue macaw

e)   Giant panda bear

**2** Now complete with the name of the animal.

a) This animal can be up to 16 meters long and weighs 40 tons. It is the h..................................................

b) This mammal can be under water for up to 5 minutes without breathing. It is the m..................................................

c) This animal lives in the tropical forest of South America. It is also known as *onça-pintada*. It is the j..................................................

d) This animal likes to fly in pairs or in groups. It is endangered because of illegal hunting. It is the b.................................................. m..................................................

## LET'S PLAY! — A Cool Trip!

**1** Let's help Millie find her clothes and accessories.

a) pink sneakers

b) black shoes

c) a pink and white cap

d) a big red schoolbag

e) a green dress

f) blue jeans

g) some colored T-shirts

# AUDIO TRANSCRIPT

## Track 7
a) Yellow
b) Pink, purple and white
c) Green
d) Brown
e) Gray and black
f) Red and black

## Track 8
a) It is a beautiful garden.
b) It is a red rose.
c) It is a big green tree.
d) It is a blue butterfly.
e) It is a red and black ladybug.
f) It is a yellow and black bee.
g) It is a brown ant.

## Track 12
On Mondays, I have fruit salad.
On Tuesdays, I have a sandwich.
On Wednesdays, I have a yogurt.
On Thursdays, I have some apple pie.
On Fridays, I have a fruit.

## Track 21
a) He's a bus driver.
b) They're doctors.
c) She's a lawyer.
d) He's an engineer.
e) They're bakers.
f) He's a postman.
g) He's a policeman.

## Track 26
a) I'm hungry. Let's go to the fast food place.
b) There is one big bookstore in this shopping mall.
c) There are two toy stores over there.
d) There is a small pet shop in this shopping mall.

## Track 27
1. It's a bus.
2. It's a car.
3. It's a motorcycle.
4. It's the subway.
5. It's a truck.
6. It's a plane.
7. It's a train.
8. It's a ship.

## Track 28

a) To go to the restaurant, go straight for two blocks on Violet Street. It's next to the post office.

b) To go to the movie theater, go straight for one block on Lily Street. It's behind the bank.

## Track 29

a) **A:** Let's go to the pet shop.
**B:** Where is the pet shop?
**A:** It's six blocks from here.
**B:** How can we get there?
**A:** On foot.

b) **A:** Let's go to the fast food place.
**B:** Where is the fast food place?
**A:** It's twelve blocks from here.
**B:** How can we get there?
**A:** By bus.

## Track 35

a) There are six humpback whales.
b) There are ten panda bears.
c) There are five gorillas.
d) There are seven loggerhead sea turtles.
e) There are eight jaguars.
f) There are nine blue macaws.
g) There are twelve manatees.
h) There are eleven golden lion tamarins.

## Track 36

a) It is a cute giant panda bear.
b) This humpback whale is a big animal.
c) The loggerhead sea turtle is a good swimmer.
d) The golden lion tamarin is a small animal.

## Track 41

a) a red dress
b) a green T-shirt
c) a pair of black shoes
d) a blue shirt
e) a pair of blue, white and gray socks

## Track 42

In Brazil:

a) Father's Day is celebrated in August.
b) Mother's Day is celebrated in March.
c) Christmas is celebrated in December.
d) Children's Day is celebrated in July.

# GLOSSARY

**A**

**a:** um, uma
**about:** sobre, acerca de
**act out:** atuar, representar
**address:** endereço
**admission ticket:** ingresso
**all through:** por todo(a)
**am:** sou; estou
**a.m.:** antes do meio-dia, de manhã
**amazing:** incrível
**an:** um, uma
**another:** outro(a)
**ant:** formiga
**anteater:** tamanduá
**apple:** maçã
**apple pie:** torta de maçã
**April:** abril
**are:** são; estão
**around:** ao redor de
**Art class:** aula de Arte
**at home:** em casa
**at least:** pelo menos
**at night:** à noite
**August:** agosto
**awesome:** incrível, fantástico

**B**

**back:** atrás, para trás
**backyard:** quintal
**bag:** mala
**baker:** padeiro(a)
**bakery:** padaria
**bamboo forest:** floresta de bambu
**bathroom:** banheiro
**be born:** nascer
**be careful:** ter cuidado
**be late:** estar atrasado(a)
**be over:** acabar
**be respectful:** ser respeitoso
**beach:** praia
**beans:** feijões
**beautiful:** bonito(a)
**because:** porque
**bedroom:** quarto
**bee:** abelha
**bell:** sino
**best:** melhor
**better:** melhor
**big:** grande
**bike:** bicicleta
**bird:** pássaro
**birth date:** data de nascimento
**birth place:** local de nascimento
**black:** preto(a)
**block:** quarteirão
**blue:** azul
**blue macaw:** arara-azul
**boat:** barco
**book:** livro
**bookstore:** livraria
**box:** caixa, quadro
**Brazilian:** brasileiro(a)
**bread:** pão
**break the code:** decifrar a mensagem
**breakfast:** café da manhã
**breathe:** respirar
**brother:** irmão
**brown:** marrom
**bug:** inseto
**bus:** ônibus
**bus driver:** motorista de ônibus
**bus stop:** ponto de ônibus
**busy:** ocupado(a)
**butterfly:** borboleta
**buy:** comprar
**by:** por, por meio de
**bye:** tchau, até logo

**C**

**can:** poder
**cap:** boné
**car:** carro
**cardboard:** cartolina, papelão
**carpool:** carona comunitária
**cart away:** recolher (lixo)
**cartoon:** desenho animado
**cat:** gato(a)
**cave:** caverna
**change:** mudar; mudança
**channel:** canal
**chart:** tabela, quadro
**cheat:** enganar, trapacear
**check:** verificar, assinalar
**choose:** escolher
**Christmas:** Natal
**circle:** circular; círculo
**city:** cidade
**classmate:** colega de turma
**climate:** clima, tempo
**climate change:** mudança climática
**clock:** relógio
**clock hand:** ponteiro de relógio
**close:** fechar
**closed:** fechado(a)
**clothes:** roupas
**collect:** coletar, pegar
**color:** cor; colorir
**colored pens:** canetas coloridas
**come:** vir
**come back:** voltar
**come on:** vamos
**comfortable:** confortável
**complete:** completar
**contemporary work:** arte contemporânea
**cookies:** biscoitos
**cooking:** cozinhar
**cool:** legal
**count:** contar
**country:** país
**credit card:** cartão de crédito
**crystal-clear:** claro(a)
**cut:** cortar
**cute:** gracioso, bonito

## D

**dad:** papai
**daily routine:** rotina diária
**daisy:** margarida
**day:** dia
**days of the week:** dias da semana
**December:** dezembro
**deliver:** entregar
**dentist:** dentista
**description:** descrição
**dessert:** sobremesa
**dining room:** sala de jantar
**dinner:** jantar
**do:** fazer
**doctor:** médico(a)
**dog:** cachorro
**doll:** boneca
**door:** porta
**draw:** desenhar
**drawing:** desenhar; desenho; desenhando
**dream house:** casa dos sonhos
**dress:** vestido
**drink:** beber; bebida
**drive:** dirigir

## E

**each:** cada
**Easter:** Páscoa
**eat:** comer
**egg:** ovo
**elderly people:** pessoas idosas
**endangered:** ameaçado(a)
**engine:** motor
**engineer:** engenheiro(a)
**environment:** meio ambiente
**environmental activist:** ativista ambiental
**every day:** todo dia
**except:** exceto
**explanation:** explicação
**extinguish fire:** apagar fogo, incêndio

## F

**fact file:** ficha técnica
**fall:** outono
**fast:** rápido(a)
**fast food place:** restaurante de comida rápida
**father:** pai
**fawn:** cervo novo, cervato
**Feasts of June:** festas juninas
**February:** fevereiro
**fewer:** menos
**find:** achar, encontrar
**fine:** bem, bom
**firefighter:** bombeiro(a)
**fish:** peixe
**floor:** chão
**floor plan:** planta baixa
**flower:** flor
**fluffy:** fofinho
**flyer:** folheto publicitário
**food:** comida, alimento(s)
**forest:** floresta
**forty-three:** quarenta e três
**forty-two:** quarenta e dois
**free of charge:** sem custo, gratuito
**French fries:** batatas fritas
**Friday:** sexta-feira
**fridge:** geladeira
**friend:** amigo(a)
**from:** de
**from here:** daqui
**fruit cake:** bolo com frutas cristalizadas
**fruit salad:** salada de frutas
**full price:** preço cheio, total
**fun:** divertir-se; diversão

## G

**game:** jogo
**garage:** garagem
**garbage:** lixo
**garbage collector:** lixeiro(a)
**garden:** jardim
**gather:** reunir, juntar
**gestation:** gestação
**girl:** menina, garota
**glass:** vidro, copo
**global warming:** aquecimento global
**glue:** colar; cola
**go:** ir
**go around:** circular, dar voltas
**go to sleep:** ir dormir
**golden lion tamarin:** mico-leão-dourado
**good:** bom, boa
**good afternoon:** boa tarde
**good evening:** boa noite
**good morning:** bom dia
**good night:** boa noite
**grandfather:** avô
**grandma:** vovó
**grandmother:** avó
**grandpa:** vovô
**grass:** grama
**gray:** cinza (cor)
**great:** grande, ótimo
**Great idea!:** Boa ideia!
**green:** verde
**grilled fish:** peixe grelhado

## H

**hair:** cabelo, pelo
**half-entry ticket:** ingresso de meia-entrada
**hang:** pendurar
**hanger rack:** arara para pendurar roupas
**happy:** feliz
**have:** ter
**have breakfast:** tomar café da manhã
**have dinner:** jantar
**have lunch:** almoçar
**head:** cabeça
**healthy:** saudável
**height:** altura
**help:** ajudar; ajuda
**her:** dela, seu

**high:** alto
**his:** dele, seu
**holiday:** feriado, férias
**home:** casa, lar
**homework:** tarefa de casa
**horn:** buzina
**hot dog:** cachorro-quente
**house:** casa
**household:** de casa, doméstico
**how:** como
**How cute!:** Que lindo!
**How many...?:** Quanto...?, Quanta...?
**humpback whale:** baleia-jubarte
**hungry:** com fome, faminto
**hurry up:** apressar-se

## I

**I:** eu
**I'm:** eu sou; eu estou
**I'm... years old:** tenho... anos
**ice cream:** sorvete de massa
**in:** em, dentro
**in cash:** pagamento em dinheiro (à vista)
**in front of:** em frente a
**indigo:** azul anil (cor)
**in pairs:** em duplas
**is:** é; está
**it:** ele, ela (animais e objetos)
**its:** seu, dele, dela (animais e objetos)

## J

**jaguar:** onça-pintada
**January:** janeiro
**job:** trabalho, emprego
**journey:** viagem
**juice:** suco
**July:** julho
**jump:** pular, saltar
**June:** junho
**jungle:** floresta
**junk food:** comida calórica e pouco nutritiva

## K

**key words:** palavras-chave
**kid:** criança
**kill:** matar
**kitchen:** cozinha
**know:** saber

## L

**lady:** senhora, senhorita
**ladybug:** joaninha
**lake:** lago
**last:** duração; durar; último(a)
**laundry room:** lavanderia
**law:** lei
**law office:** escritório de advocacia
**lawyer:** advogado(a)
**lay eggs:** botar ovos
**learn:** aprender
**leg:** perna
**let's go:** vamos
**letter:** carta; letra
**library:** biblioteca
**life:** vida
**life range:** expectativa de vida
**light:** claro(a)
**like:** gostar; como
**listen:** escutar, ouvir
**live:** viver, habitar
**living room:** sala de estar, de visita
**loggerhead sea turtle:** tartaruga-cabeçuda
**look:** olhar
**lots of:** muitos(as)
**love:** amor; amar
**lunch:** almoço

## M

**machine:** máquina
**magazine:** revista
**make:** fazer
**mammal:** mamífero
**man:** homem
**manatee:** peixe-boi
**map:** mapa
**March:** março
**marsh deer:** cervo-do-pantanal
**match:** ligar, relacionar
**May:** maio
**me:** me, mim
**meal:** comida, refeição
**means of transportation:** meios de transporte
**mechanic:** mecânico(a)
**menu:** cardápio
**milk:** leite
**mime game:** jogo de mímica
**mine:** meu(s), minha(s)
**miss:** faltar
**model:** modelo, maquete
**mom:** mamãe
**Monday:** segunda-feira
**monster:** monstro
**month:** mês
**more than:** mais do que
**most used:** mais usado
**mostly:** principalmente; em geral
**mother:** mãe
**motorcycle:** motocicleta, moto
**mountain:** montanha
**move:** mover, mudar
**Ms.:** senhora, senhorita
**my:** meu, minha

## N

**name:** nome
**nature:** natureza
**near:** perto
**need:** precisar
**neighbor:** vizinho(a)
**neighborhood:** vizinhança
**new:** novo(a)
**night:** noite
**no:** não
**non-profit:** sem fins lucrativos
**not:** não
**November:** novembro
**now:** agora
**number:** número; numerar
**nut:** noz, castanha

## O

**oatmeal:** aveia
**occupation:** profissão, ocupação
**ocean:** oceano, mar
**o'clock:** hora exata
**October:** outubro
**on:** em, sobre
**on foot:** a pé
**open:** abrir; aberto(a)
**open air museum:** museu ao ar livre
**orange juice:** suco de laranja
**order:** ordem, sequência
**other:** outro(a)
**otter:** lontra
**our:** nosso(s), nossa(s)
**out:** fora, para fora
**outside:** fora, do lado de fora
**owned:** que pertence a

## P

**pack:** fazer as malas
**panda bear:** panda
**pants:** calça
**parcel:** pacote
**parents:** pais ou responsáveis
**park:** parque
**pasta:** massa (macarrão)
**patient:** paciente
**pay:** pagar
**payment:** pagamento
**people:** pessoas
**physician:** médico(a)
**piano lesson:** aula de piano
**picture:** imagem, fotografia
**pieces:** peças
**pink:** cor-de-rosa
**place:** lugar
**plane:** avião
**plastic bottle:** garrafa de plástico
**play:** brincar, jogar, tocar
**play area:** local para brincar
**please:** por favor
**p.m.:** depois do meio-dia, à tarde
**point:** apontar
**policeman:** policial masculino
**policewoman:** policial feminina
**pollution:** poluição
**postman:** carteiro
**postwoman:** carteira
**potato:** batata
**practice:** prática; praticar
**practitioner of medicine:** médico(a)
**purple:** roxo(a)
**put:** pôr, colocar

## Q

**qualified:** qualificado(a)
**question:** pergunta; perguntar
**quickly:** rápido, rapidamente

## R

**rainbow:** arco-íris
**read:** ler
**ready:** pronto
**red:** vermelho(a)
**reduce:** reduzir
**repair:** consertar
**reptile:** réptil
**research:** pesquisa; pesquisar
**respect:** respeito; respeitar
**rest:** descansar
**rewrite:** reescrever
**rice:** arroz
**ride a bike:** andar de bicicleta
**riddle:** jogo de adivinhação, charada
**ring:** soar; tocar
**roasted chicken:** frango assado
**room:** sala, cômodo
**rose:** rosa
**round:** em torno de; roda
**run:** correr

## S

**same:** o mesmo, a mesma
**sand:** areia
**sandwich:** sanduíche
**Saturday:** sábado
**sausage:** salsicha, linguiça
**save:** poupar
**say:** dizer
**schedule:** horário, programação
**school:** escola
**schoolbag:** mochila escolar
**school bus:** ônibus escolar
**school holidays:** férias escolares
**scissors:** tesoura
**scooter:** patinete
**sea turtle:** tartaruga marinha
**search:** procurar, pesquisar
**season:** estação do ano
**see:** ver
**September:** setembro
**sequence:** sequência
**share:** compartilhar, dividir
**ship:** navio
**shirt:** camisa
**shoes:** sapatos
**shopping mall:** *shopping center*
**short:** baixo(a), curto(a)
**silly:** bobo, tolo
**since:** desde
**sing:** cantar
**singer:** cantor(a)
**sister:** irmã
**skirt:** saia
**sky:** céu
**sleep:** dormir
**slow:** devagar
**small:** pequeno(a)
**snack:** lanche, petisco
**sneakers:** tênis (calçado)

**socks:** meias
**soda:** refrigerante
**some:** algum, alguns
**someone:** alguém
**sometimes:** às vezes, algumas vezes
**sorry:** desculpe(-me)
**species:** espécie
**spider's web:** teia de aranha
**spring:** primavera
**start:** começar
**stay:** ficar
**stick:** colar
**Stockholm:** Estocolmo
**stop:** parar; pare
**store:** loja
**street:** rua
**stroll:** passear, dar uma volta
**student:** estudante, aluno(a)
**study:** estudar
**subway:** metrô
**summer:** verão
**sun:** sol
**Sunday:** domingo
**sunflower:** girassol
**surfboard:** prancha de surfe
**surf shop:** loja de artigos para surfe
**sweater:** malha de lã
**Sweden:** Suécia
**sweet:** doce

## T

**tail:** rabo, cauda
**tall:** alto(a)
**take:** pegar, tomar
**Take care!:** Cuide-se!
**taste:** gosto; ter gosto de
**teach:** ensinar
**teacher:** professor(a)
**teen:** adolescente
**telephone number:** número do telefone
**thank you:** obrigado (a você)
**that:** aquele, aquela, aquilo
**the:** o, a, os, as

**the largest:** o(a) maior
**their:** deles, delas
**them:** os, as
**there:** lá
**these:** estes, estas
**think:** pensar
**this:** este, esta, isto
**through:** através de, por
**Thursday:** quinta-feira
**time:** tempo, hora
**to:** para
**toast:** torrada
**today:** hoje
**too:** muito; também
**town:** cidade, vilarejo
**toy:** brinquedo
**toy store:** loja de brinquedos
**train:** trem
**train station:** estação de trem
**trash:** lixo
**travel:** viajar
**tree:** árvore
**trip:** viagem
**T-shirt:** camiseta
**Tuesday:** terça-feira
**tuna sandwich:** sanduíche de atum
**turkey breast:** peito de peru

## U

**under:** sob, embaixo de
**underground:** metrô
**unscramble:** desembaralhar
**up and down:** para cima e para baixo
**usually:** geralmente

## V

**vegetables:** legumes, verduras
**very:** muito
**visit:** visitar
**vowel:** vogal

## W

**wait:** esperar

**wake up:** despertar, acordar
**walk:** andar
**want:** querer
**warrior:** guerreiro(a)
**watch cartoons:** assistir a desenho animado
**water:** água
**waterfall:** cachoeira, cascata
**wear:** vestir; usar
**weather:** tempo, clima
**Wednesday:** quarta-feira
**week:** semana
**weight:** peso
**went out:** saiu
**wetland:** pantanal
**what:** que, qual
**wheels:** rodas
**when:** quando
**where:** onde
**white:** branco(a)
**who:** quem
**why:** por que
**wildlife:** vida selvagem
**window:** janela
**wing:** asa
**winter:** inverno
**wiper:** limpador de para--brisa
**word:** palavra
**word cloud:** nuvem de palavras
**work:** trabalho; trabalhar
**work of art:** obra de arte
**world:** mundo
**write:** escrever

## Y

**years old:** anos de idade
**yellow:** amarelo(a)
**yes:** sim
**young:** jovem
**your:** seu(s), sua(s)
**yourself:** você mesmo(a), si mesmo
**yummy:** delicioso(a)

## Z

**zoo:** zoológico

# SUGGESTIONS FOR STUDENTS

## • Books

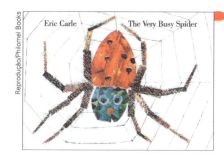

Eric Carle. **The Very Busy Spider**. New York: Philomel Books, 1995.

Certa manhã, o vento traz uma pequena aranha pelo campo. Ela tece sua teia em uma cerca. Os animais da fazenda, um a um, tentam distraí-la, mas a pequena aranha continua fazendo seu trabalho. Quando a aranha termina a teia, é capaz de mostrar a todos os animais que sua criação é bonita e também bastante útil!

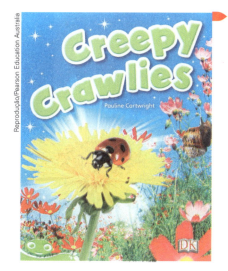

Pauline Cartwright. **Green:** Creepy Crawlies. Austrália: Pearson Education Limited, 2010.

Conheça os *Creepy Crawlies*, pequenos animais rastejantes e estranhos que podem viver em seu jardim, na sua casa e até mesmo em... você. Esse livro traz informações interessantes sobre o corpo desses pequenos animais, bem como características e curiosidades peculiares de cada um deles.

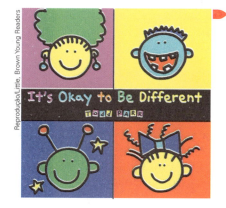

Todd Parr. **It's Okay to Be Different**. Austrália: Little, Brown Young Readers Education, 2016.

*It's Okay to Be Different* (Tudo bem ser diferente) transmite, de maneira brilhante e acessível, mensagens importantes de aceitação, compreensão e confiança para crianças. O livro apresenta cores fortes e brilhantes e cenas simples que fizeram de Todd Parr uma voz importante na literatura infantil. Esse livro vai inspirar as crianças a celebrar sua individualidade por meio da aceitação dos outros e da autoconfiança – e a entender que nunca é cedo para desenvolver uma autoestima saudável.

## Sites

▶ www.wordhippo.com

O Wordhippo é um *site* educativo que oferece vários aplicativos relacionados a palavras, inclusive um dicionário *on-line* completo. Você poderá encontrar sinônimos, antônimos, frases com exemplos de uso contextualizado da palavra, além de rimas e pronúncia. Uma excelente ferramenta para desenvolver a aquisição de vocabulário novo.

▶ www.vocabulary.co.il

Esse *site* dispõe de uma grande variedade de jogos para estimular a aquisição de vocabulário novo por meio de jogos educativos e oferece uma forma divertida e prazerosa de dinamizar a aula.

▶ www.dreamenglish.com

O *site* Dream English tem como objetivo levar às crianças músicas e vídeos educacionais simples que abordam vocabulário e as principais estruturas gramaticais de forma prazerosa e lúdica.

Acesso em: abr. 2020.

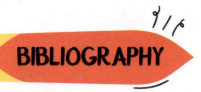

## BIBLIOGRAPHY

ALMEIDA FILHO, J. C. P. *Dimensões comunicativas no ensino de línguas*. 2. ed. Campinas: Pontes, 2000.

BRASIL. Base Nacional Comum Curricular (BNCC). Brasília: MEC, 2018. Disponível em: <http://basenacionalcomum.mec.gov.br/>. Acesso em: 26 set. 2019.

CELANI, M. A. A. *Ensino de segunda língua*: redescobrindo as origens. São Paulo: Educ., 1997.

HARMER, J. *The Practice of English Language Teaching*. 4. ed. London: Pearson Longman, 2007.

MOITA LOPES, L. P. A nova ordem mundial, os Parâmetros Curriculares Nacionais e o ensino de inglês no Brasil. A base intelectual para uma ação política. In: BARBARA, L.; RAMOS, R. de C. G. *Reflexão e ações no ensino-aprendizagem de línguas*. São Paulo: Mercado de Letras, 2003.

VYGOTSKY, L. S. *A formação social da mente*: o desenvolvimento dos processos psicológicos superiores. São Paulo: Martins Fontes, 1991.

# The Super Ecohero

Eliete Canesi Morino
Rita Brugin de Faria

Aluno: ....................................................................................................
Escola: ............................................................... Turma: ............................

editora scipione